JOYFUL LIVING
FINDING JOY IN LITTLE THINGS

LI-LING OOI

BAILBROOK LANE

COPYRIGHT

All rights reserved. No part of this publication may be reproduced, stored in a retrieval system, or transmitted, in any form, or by any means, without the prior permission in writing of Bailbrook Lane, or as expressly permitted by law, or under terms agreed with the appropriate reprographics rights organisation.

You must not circulate this book in any other binding or cover and you must impose the same condition on any acquirer.

Enquiries concerning reproduction outside the scope of the above should be sent to enquiries@bailbrooklane.com

The moral rights of the author have been asserted.

© Li-ling Ooi

First published 2023

Published in the United Kingdom

Ooi, Li-ling

Joyful Living - Finding Joy in Little Things / Li-ling Ooi.

Paperback ISBN 978-1-913557-05-8

Ebook ISBN 978-1-913557-04-1

Bailbrook Lane is an imprint of Xelium Ltd.

DISCLAIMER

The information provided in this book, "Joyful Living - Finding Joy in Little Things" is for general informational purposes only and is not intended as, nor should it be considered a substitute for, professional medical advice or individual counselling.

While the author and publisher have made every effort to ensure that the information in this book was correct at the time of publication, the author and publisher do not assume and hereby disclaim any liability to any party for any loss, damage, or disruption caused by errors or omissions, whether such errors or omissions result from negligence, accident, or any other cause.

This book is not intended as a substitute for professional advice or treatment. The reader is advised to consult with a professional or a specialised individual for any particular query or issues. The author and publisher specifically disclaim all responsibility for any liability, loss or risk, personal or otherwise, which is incurred as a consequence, directly or indirectly, of the use and application of any of the contents of this book.

CONTENTS

Foreword — vi
How to Use This Book — viii
Invitation — xi

1. Introduction to Joyful Living — 1
2. Mindful Awareness — 11
3. Nature's Beauty — 24
4. Everyday Moments: Making the Ordinary Extraordinary — 41
5. Meaningful Connections: The Joy in Togetherness — 51
6. Simple Pleasures — 60
7. Gratitude and Appreciation — 67
8. Letting Go of Expectations — 75
9. Overcoming Obstacles and Building Resilience — 84
10. Creating your Joyful Life — 99
11. Reflection and Celebration — 110

References — 117
Acknowledgements — 121

About the Author — 122
Join my mailing list — 123
Also by Li-ling Ooi — 124
Please leave a review — 125
Coming soon — 126

FOREWORD

In a world that never stops, where the pursuit of the extraordinary can overshadow the beauty of the ordinary, we find ourselves on a journey to tap into a precious and timeless treasure: joy. This book *Joyful Living - Finding Joy in Little Things*, serves as a reminder and a guide for us on this journey of rediscovering the magic that lies in the simplest of moments.

Amidst the hectic demands of modern life, we often overlook the small pleasures that are present in our everyday. We so often forget that joy is not confined to grand achievements or momentous occasions but rather, it is nestled in the whispers of nature, the laughter of loved ones, and the quiet moments of self-reflection.

As you journey through the pages of this book, you are invited to explore the art of mindful living, where every breath becomes an opportunity to embrace the present moment. You will be encouraged to participate in the wisdom of cultivating gratitude, savour life's multitude of flavours, form and nurture connections and relationships that enrich all of our lives.

Joyful Living is not meant to be just a book; it is a lived experience of adopting and practising a new outlook. Each chapter reveals a new perspective of joy, guiding you through the exploration of simple pleasures, the art of mindful awareness, and the great impact of kindness and gratitude. It gently reminds us that joy is not a distant destination but a path we can tread right now, right where we are.

The words within these pages are a gentle reminder that joy is not an elusive butterfly to be chased after but a garden to be grown and nurtured within ourselves. The journey to joy is a journey within, a journey of self-discovery, of slowing down to savour all life's different experiences, and of opening our hearts to the beauty that surrounds us.

As you immerse yourself in the insights, reflections, and practices shared in this book, may you uncover the hidden gems of joy that have always been within your reach. May you find new inspiration to embark on your own journey of discovery, to seek joy in the everyday, and to embrace the art of joyful mindful living with open arms.

We are delighted to present to you *Joyful Living - Finding Joy in Little Things*. May its wisdom bring a touch of serenity, a spark of delight, and a renewed sense of wonder into your life. Let its pages guide you towards a more meaningful existence, where the little things shine with extraordinary brilliance, and joy becomes an ever-present companion on your journey.

With love and joy,
   Li-ling

HOW TO USE THIS BOOK

Dear Reader,

Welcome to a journey of discovery and reflection! As they always say, we write the books that we ourselves truly need to read. This is no less true of Joyful Living. This book has been written to serve as both a guide and a companion on my own journey to a joy-filled life.

In order to make the most of this book, this is what I would recommend:

1. Embrace the Journey

There is no rush. Whether you choose to read this book cover to cover or jump between the chapters or even the sections, remember that the journey to finding joy is deeply personal. Use this book in any way that feels right to you.

2. Reflect and internalise

At the end of the various sections, you'll find thought-provoking questions and reflective prompts. Take your time to reflect, consider and ponder over them. Perhaps keep a journal alongside to write down your thoughts and observations.

3. Practice mindfully

Throughout the book, you'll come across practical exercises designed to help you tune in to life's seemingly insignificant joys - small moments that would typically pass on by. Don't just read about them—practice! As with any skill, seeking joy in your every day will become more intuitive with mindful regular practice.

4. Revisit regularly

This book isn't meant to be read once and then shelved. As you grow and evolve, you will no doubt find different insights that resonate with you at different points of your life. Come back and reread sections whenever you need a gentle reminder or a fresh perspective.

5. Share and discuss

If something from this book resonates with you, please do talk about it! And tell me - I would love to hear how the book has made a difference in your life! You could also share your insights with friends, family, or join a discussion group. Sharing personal experiences can enrich your journey and provide valuable community support.

6. Create a joyful environment

Consider setting aside a dedicated space for reading and reflecting—a cozy corner with a comfortable chair, soft lighting, perhaps with a cup of tea or coffee at hand. As you settle yourself into a calming, peaceful space, approach the ideas and suggestions in this book with an open mind and an open heart.

7. Stay open

Some concepts may feel familiar, while others might challenge your current perspectives. Approach each chapter with an open heart and mind, allowing the book to guide, inspire, and perhaps even occasionally challenge you.

Finally, remember that the journey to finding joy in little things is a continuous process. There will be days filled with exciting discoveries, and others where the world seems dull and boring. But with each page you turn and each exercise you practise, you are taking a step closer to recognising, embracing, and celebrating the little joys that can be found all around you.

Happy reading and joyful living!

INVITATION
JOIN THE 7-DAY JOURNEY TO JOYFUL LIVING

The Journey to Joyful Living is a 7-day journey reminding us of the little things we can practise and do each day to help embrace the little joys in our lives. To share and encourage each other on the path to Joyful Living, I have created a 7-day journey so that we can all learn, consider and share our experiences on this journey to Joyful Living.

Our journey together consists of a daily email sent to your Inbox for 7 days encouraging you to take active, purposeful steps towards finding joy in little things.

Each day's email is linked to a page on my website, where you can download resources, and share your experiences, ideas and thoughts in the comments section.

Sign up to join the 7 day Journey to Joyful Living online at

www.lilingooi.com/7dayjoy

I am so excited to share this journey towards Joyful Living with you.

Li-ling

1
INTRODUCTION TO JOYFUL LIVING

Joy is what happens to us when we allow ourselves to recognise how good things really are.

— MARIANNE WILLIAMSON

Life in the modern world is typically defined by a never-ending pursuit of success, often at the cost of our own emotional well-being. We chase professional accomplishments, material wealth, and societal approval, neglecting the little moments of happiness that make life truly worthwhile. This book is an invitation to a different perspective—a life infused with joy, rooted in a deep appreciation of the everyday and embracing optimism and enthusiasm. It is not about ignoring the challenges that life presents, but rather finding joy among them and celebrating life in all its messy glory.

Questions for self-reflection
1. How often do I pause to recognise and savour moments of joy in my everyday life?
2. In what ways has the pursuit of success or societal approval overshadowed moments of genuine happiness in my life?

THE CONCEPT OF JOY AND ITS SIGNIFICANCE

Before we begin our exploration into joyful living, it is essential to understand what joy means. Joy is more than just a transient feeling or a momentary sensation of happiness; it is a deep, enduring state of being that permeates every aspect of our lives. Unlike happiness, which is often dependent on external circumstances, joy springs from within, nourished by our innermost thoughts, attitudes, and perspectives.

In psychology, joy is considered one of the fundamental positive emotions that contribute to our overall well-being. It has been linked to numerous benefits,[1] including increased life satisfaction, better physical health, improved mental resilience, and even enhanced creativity. When we infuse our lives with joy, we do not merely exist; we thrive.

At its core, joy is an internal state that arises from within us, independent of external circumstances. It is not dependent on material possessions, achievements, or specific life events. Instead, joy is a deeply rooted sense of well-being that can be cultivated and experienced in any situation, regardless of the external factors.

One of the key aspects of understanding joy is recognising that it is not a destination to be reached but a way of staying in the present moment. It is not something we need to pursue or chase after; rather, it is something we can tap into and develop within ourselves.

Joy is often associated with a sense of gratitude and appreciation for the present moment. It involves fully embracing and savouring the experiences, connections, and beauty that surround us. By changing our focus from what is lacking to what is abundant in our lives, we open ourselves up to the potential for joy.

And while joy can arise from extraordinary experiences or significant life events, it is important to note that joy can also be found in the little things. It is in the everyday moments, simple pleasures, and ordinary experiences where joy often resides. It can be found in a warm cup of coffee on a chilly morning, the laughter of loved ones, the beauty of nature, or even in a quiet moment of solitude.

Understanding joy requires a shift in perspective. It involves letting go of the constant pursuit of external achievements and learning to find contentment and delight in the present moment. It is about recognising that joy is not a result of external circumstances, but rather an internal state of being that we can tune into at any time.

Tuning in to joy involves developing a mindset of appreciation, gratitude and positivity. It is about shifting our focus towards the blessings, opportunities, and small moments of joy that exist in our lives. By practicing gratitude and appreciating the little things, we create a foundation for joy to flourish.

Questions for self-reflection
1. Can you recall a moment when you felt genuine joy regardless of any external circumstances?

2. How might focussing on a deeper sense of internal joy impact your well-being and perspective on life?

EMBRACING YOUR OWN EXPERIENCE OF JOY

Each one of us experiences joy in unique and individual ways. What is important is to recognise each of these occasions and moments when joy does arrive. Try and remember and recall the feeling and the emotions associated with your physical surroundings, particularly a place where you felt freedom or happiness, or perhaps your feeling of joy is associated with a particular moment or even a special insight. Take a moment to try and recall and recapture the essence of that experience and emotion.

Being in wide-open landscapes especially near the sea is especially awe-inspiring and breath-taking for me. The very first time I noticed this feeling of awe was on Skomer Island in Wales, UK as we were trampling along the footpaths of the island. We were there during the puffins' nesting season and because it was such a secluded spot, the birds were not wary nor afraid of our presence. We managed to walk amongst their burrowing nests, watch wild rabbits munching their way through the long grasses and spy on seals in the harbour.

The realisation that I was but a tiny speck in the grand scheme of the world, also made me aware that no matter how small we are, our contributions remain immensely important.

Similarly, flowers are especially fascinating to me. I love peering into the 'heart' of each one, at each stage of their growth process. I am enchanted by how automated the process is. No one tells the flower what to do or how to do it. The knowledge and information seem innate, driven by bio-chemical processes within the flower and the plant.

Whatever and however your joy is triggered, it is a gift to be aware of when you are experiencing it. Take a moment to pause and if possible, identify a couple of moments that bring you or have brought you joy.

Questions for self-reflection
1. What are some unique triggers or experiences that consistently bring you joy?
2. How can you incorporate reminders of these joy-inducing memories into your daily life?

FINDING JOY IN LITTLE THINGS

In our busy lives, as we find ourselves chasing ever larger milestones, grander achievements, and more significant events we forget that it is in the small moments, the seemingly insignificant instances that occur throughout our day, where true joy and fulfilment reside. The power of these small moments lies in their ability to bring us immense happiness, contentment, and a deeper appreciation for life.

Small moments have the power to anchor us in the present. When we slow down and fully engage with the seemingly mundane aspects of our lives, we cultivate mindfulness and presence. Whether it is simply savouring the aroma of freshly brewed coffee, feeling the warmth of sunlight on our skin, or relishing a quiet moment of solitude, these small moments awaken us to the richness of the present moment. They remind us to pause, breathe, and truly experience life as it unfolds.

The small moments of our daily routines offer countless opportunities for joy. It could be the simple pleasure of sharing a genuine smile with a stranger, discovering a beautifully blooming flower during a walk, or relishing a delicious meal. These moments may seem insignificant on their own, but when we intentionally seek and appreciate them, they have the power to fill our hearts with immense joy. Finding joy in the little things allows us to infuse our lives with positivity and gratitude, enhancing our overall well-being.

Small moments have the potential to deepen our connections with others. Engaging in heartfelt conversations, sharing laughter, or offering acts of kindness in small, meaningful ways can create lasting bonds and strengthen relationships. It is these small moments that we often find the most genuine expressions of love, support, and understanding. By valuing and cherishing these small moments, we nurture the connections that bring joy and meaning to our lives.

While monumental events may leave a lasting impact on our lives, it is the accumulation of small moments that shapes our most cherished memories. These moments, when strung together, form the true value of our lives. Reflecting on the simple joys experienced during ordinary days can evoke a sense of nostalgia and gratitude. It is these memories that are a source of comfort, inspiration, and a reminder of the beauty that resides within the small moments of life.

The power of small moments lies in their ability to awaken us to the present, infuse our lives with joy, deepen our connections, and create lasting memories. By focussing our awareness and appreciation for these seemingly insignificant instances, we can learn to find a deeper sense of fulfilment and find beauty in the ordinary.

Questions for self-reflection
1. What small moments or rituals already bring you joy, and how can you be more intentional about recognising them?
2. How can you create space in your daily routine to pause and appreciate the little things?

SMALL MOMENT OF JOY RITUALS

Building on small rituals throughout your day can help ground you and help you be more aware and open to the calm and joy that surrounds your day-to-day life. When you take time to practise a momentary ritual, whether it is a quiet pause a lunch time, or lighting a candle first thing in the morning, an intentional action or ritual can often remind us to bring our attention to the present moment, to be thankful and appreciate all that we have.

Questions for self-reflection
1. What simple rituals could you introduce into your day to help anchor in moments of joy?
2. How might these rituals serve as a buffer or reset during more challenging days?

THE BENEFITS OF FINDING JOY IN LITTLE THINGS

There's a well-known saying, "Enjoy the little things in life, for one day you may look back and realise they were the big things." This speaks to the heart of joyful living. It's about finding delight in the simple, ordinary moments that fill our days—the warmth of the morning sun on our face, the scent of freshly brewed coffee, a good book, a child's laughter, or even the quiet solitude of a peaceful night.

When we begin to notice and appreciate these little things, we unlock a constant source of joy that is independent of life's fluctuations. In fact, research shows that individuals who regularly acknowledge and appreciate the positive aspects of life, however small, tend to be more resilient in the face of stress and adversity[2]. They also attest to greater life satisfaction, confirming that the practice of savouring small joys can lead to a substantial increase in overall well-being.

> Questions for self-reflection
> 1. How has taking time to savour the small moments impacted your emotional resilience in the past?
> 2. In what ways can you make it a habit to celebrate the seemingly insignificant joys in your life?

CHOOSING MINDSET OF GRATITUDE AND POSITIVITY

An essential part of the joyful living lies in purposefully choosing a positive mindset—a lens through which we view our experiences, relationships, and even ourselves. A positive mindset doesn't mean ignoring life's challenges or glossing over painful emotions. Instead, it involves acknowledging these difficulties while also focusing on strengths and opportunities.

A powerful tool for fostering positivity is the practice of gratitude. When we appreciate what we have, we shift our attention from lack and loss to abundance and gain. Regularly expressing gratitude can help us develop a positive outlook, reduce stress, improve our relationships, and boost our overall satisfaction with life.

So, how do we practice gratitude? It can be as simple as maintaining a daily journal where we write down three things, we are thankful for each day. It could also involve expressing appreciation to others more often or even just spending a few quiet moments each day reflecting on the aspects of life that bring us joy.

In her book Braiding Sweetgrass[3], Robin Kimmerer explains how her father always gave thanks first to the land, by pouring the first cup of coffee and making an offering of it to the land. In a similar way, saying grace and giving thanks before eating akin to the Japanese tradition of saying *itadakimasu* before every meal, brings our focus to the practise of gratitude and thankfulness.

The journey to joyful living isn't about dramatic transformations or monumental leaps, it is in the small, consistent steps—pausing to appreciate the little joys, practicing gratitude, and choosing to focus on a positive outlook. Over time, these tiny shifts in perception and attitude can lead to a profound change in our overall experience of life.

By living joyfully, we do not merely survive life's storms—we learn to dance in the rain. This chapter is merely an introduction to this enriching journey, offering you tools and insights to embark on your path to joyful living. As we move on into the subsequent chapters, we will explore more strategies and practices that will help you infuse your life with joy, resilience, and well-being.

At its core, joy is a profound and lasting emotion that goes beyond fleeting happiness. Understanding joy requires recognising that it is an internal state of being. It can be found in the ordinary moments of life and is closely tied to gratitude, appreciation, and a positive mindset. By embracing joy and allowing it in our lives, we open ourselves up to a more fulfilling and meaningful existence.

Questions for self-reflection
1. How frequently do you express gratitude for the positive aspects of your life?
2. Are there specific tools or practices you can incorporate to foster a more consistent positive and grateful outlook?

2

MINDFUL AWARENESS

The miracle is not to walk on water. The miracle is to walk on the green earth, dwelling deeply in the present moment and feeling truly alive.

— THICH NHAT HAHN

In the constant rush of our modern lives, it is easy to overlook the everyday joys that permeate throughout our days. The ordinary can become boring and repetitive, and we can easily lose sight of the joyful lifts that ordinary simple moments might provide. This chapter focuses on how we can use mindful awareness to rediscover and relish these joyful moments; observing the world with fresh eyes and maintaining calm amidst life's chaos.

PRACTICING MINDFULNESS TO ENHANCE PRESENT-MOMENT AWARENESS

The ancient Buddhist practice of mindfulness has gained prominence in recent years as an effective way to manage stress, improve mental health, and increase happiness[1]. But more importantly, mindfulness serves as a key that unlocks the ability to fully experience and savour life's everyday moments.

WHAT IS MINDFULNESS?

Mindfulness, at its core, is a simple concept. It is about being fully present in the moment, consciously aware of our thoughts, feelings, sensations, and the environment around us. To simply be aware of ourselves and the happenings around us without any pre-conceived notions or judgement. The practise of mindfulness is about letting go of ruminations about the past or worries about the future, and instead focusing entirely on the here and now.

When we practice mindfulness, we observe our life as it unfolds, moment by moment. We pay attention to our experiences rather than getting caught up in automatic reactions, ideas and judgements about how it 'should' be. Practising mindfulness encourages us to be purposeful in our thoughts and our actions as we go about our every day; helping to ensure that we do not respond by simply being on 'autopilot.'

As we practise being aware and mindful in our everyday life and in each moment, we begin to open ourselves up to the joy of being fully engaged with the present.

HOW TO PRACTICE MINDFULNESS

1. Mindful Breathing

Mindful breathing is one of the most fundamental practices of mindfulness. It involves directing your attention to breath—the inhalations and exhalations, the rhythm, the sensation of the air passing through your nostrils or your chest rising and falling. You do not need to change the way you breathe; you simply observe it as it is. When your mind wanders—and it inevitably will—gently bring your attention back to the breath. This practice not only anchors you in the present moment but also has a calming effect on your mind.

While it is often used as an early practise to learning meditation, mindful breathing can take place anywhere and at any time. Each time you notice yourself becoming more tense or more stressed, or when things are feeling out of your control, bring your attention back to your breath. Notice how your chest expands and fills up with air as you breathe in, and contracts as you breathe out expelling all the breath from your lungs. A few minutes of this gentle awareness and observation of your breathing will lower your heart-rate, pulse, reduce your anxiety and improve your mood and mental state.[2]

2. Mindful Observation

From mindful breathing, extend your mindfulness practice to your senses. Notice the sounds, smells, tastes, tactile sensations, and sights around you. Pay attention to the familiar and seemingly mundane aspects of life in a new way —the aroma of your coffee, the sensation of water on your skin while showering, the colours of a sunrise. This practice helps us focus on being present in the activity that we are doing.

Observing and paying attention to the details of your everyday activities helps to ensure that your mind is not wandering off by itself, creating scenarios and making up stories. Instead, by being mindfully present and observing each activity as you perform it, it enables you to appreciate not just the contribution of each material activity or object, but also allows you to be aware of the wonder of your own abilities and gifts.

For example, when you take a moment to smell a perfumed flower, you learn not only appreciate the scent, but you might also become aware of the gentle colouring of each flower, and the texture of each petal. You might become observant to the function of each flower, its role in nature and its purpose in enhancing its own species. You may also eventually come to realise and contemplate the wonder of your own ability to smell, touch and observe each of these wonders of nature.

3. Mindful Activities

Similarly, you can bring mindfulness into any activity you do. Whether you're eating, walking, washing dishes, or brushing your teeth, try to do it with full awareness. Notice each movement, the sensations, and your interaction with your environment. Engage fully with the task at hand, and try to do it slowly and deliberately. This transforms a routine activity into a mindful practice, grounding you in the present.

Revered monk Thich Nat Hahn[3] reminds us "If while

washing dishes, we think only of the cup of tea that awaits us, thus hurrying to get the dishes out of the way as if they were a nuisance, then we are not "washing the dishes to wash the dishes."What's more, we are not alive during the time we are washing the dishes. In fact, we are completely incapable of realizing the miracle of life while standing at the sink."

Mindfulness when practised continuously becomes more than just a technique—it is a way of life. It becomes about cultivating a purposeful, intentional relationship with each and every one of your experiences, while staying present, open, and curious in each moment. With regular practice, mindfulness will increase your capacity for intentional living, purposeful joy and a greater appreciation of life.

Questions for self-reflection
1. How does the pace of your daily life affect your ability to stay present, and what steps can you take to slow down and be more mindful?
2. When you notice your mind wandering, what strategies can you employ to gently guide it back to the present moment?

THE BENEFITS OF MINDFULNESS

Practicing mindfulness is known to reduce stress and anxiety, improve focus and memory, enhance emotional resilience, and promote a sense of peace and well-being.[4] Being mindful in our everyday lives allows us to break free from negative thought patterns and react more purposefully to situations. But perhaps one of the most profound benefits of mindfulness is its ability to enhance our capacity for joy. In focusing on the present moment, we create the space to appreciate and savour life's simple pleasures, transforming the ordinary into the extraordinary.

Incorporating mindfulness into our daily routine might seem daunting at first, but with practice, it becomes a natural part of our life. As we continue to cultivate mindfulness, we find that every moment holds the potential for joy and happiness. We just need to be present to experience it.

OBSERVE THE WORLD WITH FRESH EYES AND AN OPEN HEART

In the practise of mindful awareness, it is crucial to look at the world with what Zen Buddhists call a "beginner's mind". This means approaching each moment as if you're experiencing it for the first time, free from preconceived notions and judgments. By doing this, we open ourselves to a world rich with wonders that often go unnoticed.

Try to adopt this mindset as you go about your day. Revel in the warmth of the sun, the cool breeze on your face, the laughter of a child, or the aroma of your favourite meal. Let yourself be moved by the beauty in the everyday, and let it fill you with joy.

TECHNIQUES FOR STAYING GROUNDED AMIDST CHAOS

In the whirlwind of life, it is very easy to become entangled in stresses, pressures, and difficulties. These inevitable aspects of existence can distract us from the present moment, causing anxiety, restlessness, and even despair.

Amidst the chaos, we can make use of different strategies to help us stay grounded and connected with our inner peace. Here, are a series of techniques to regain our balance and find tranquillity when we are caught up in turbulent times.

1. Breathing Exercises – 4-7-8 breathing

The breath serves as an ever-present anchor to the present moment. When you feel overwhelmed, consciously shift your focus to your breath. Engage in slow, deep breaths, inhaling for 4 seconds deeply through your nose, holding it for 7 seconds, then releasing your breath slowly for 8 seconds, through your mouth. You can breathe this way for as long as you need to or if you prefer, you can set aside time (5 minutes a day) specifically to practise this.

This method of breathing is known to have a calming effect on the nervous system. Mindfully breathing in this way can help refocus your mind, reduce stress and calm the nervous system.

2. Body Scan Meditation

The body scan is another mindfulness technique that encourages us to check-in with our bodies and bring awareness to different physical sensations.

Set aside 10-15 minutes before embarking on this practise. This type of body scan is best done while lying down either on your bed or on your yoga mat. Start at one end of your body, such as your toes, and slowly move your focus through each part of your body, noting any sensations, tension, or discomfort. As you move through each part of your body, take the opportunity to check in with the sensations and insights that might arise automatically for you. Take your time and slowly clench and purposefully relax each part of your body in turn as you scan through your body.

This technique will help you become fully present in your body, grounding you in the here and now. When you reach the very tip of your head, assuming you started at your toes, take some time to purposefully relax into your body. Breathe slowly and deeply. Taking time to notice any sensations that arise. If your limbs feel heavy, take time to relax for a while.

3. Mindful Walking

The practice of mindful walking is about being fully aware and present during the simple act of walking. As you walk, bring your attention to the sensations in your feet as they make contact with the ground, the movement of your muscles, the air against your skin, and the sounds around you. Be fully aware of each step that you take as you take it. Be aware of how your body feels in the environment and what you can see and feel as you take each step

Mindful walking much like the mindful activities and mindful observations discussed in the earlier section, requires that we withhold judgement and we simply attend to being present through whatever activity it is that we are engaged in. Mindful walking, whether simply a short trip from the living room to the kitchen or a more purposeful walk or hike in nature insists that we focus entirely on the action of walking, as we walk. The placement of each step, the awareness of our breath, the ease and flow of each through our nostrils and our chest, the smoothness or strenuosity of each stride. Being mindful as we walk, allows us to stay in the present focussed only on the activity of walking.

4. Five Senses Exercise 5-4-3-2-1 grounding technique

This grounding technique is a quick and effective way to bring your focus back to the present when you feel overwhelmed.

Pause and observe your surroundings, then acknowledge
a) five things you can see,
b) four things you can touch,
c) three things you can hear,
d) two things you can smell, and
e) one thing you can taste.

This exercise is aimed at helping you to tune into your immediate sensory experiences, drawing your attention to your senses and surroundings. Instead of being caught up in whatever drama or unwanted narrative is playing and replaying in your head, using the five senses exercise makes us bring our focus back to our immediate surroundings (awareness) and then appreciate our ability to use each of our senses in turn (gratitude) which in turn helps to allow us to tune to each moment's grace, regardless of the circumstances in which we find ourselves.

5. Mindful Journaling

Writing often serves as a powerful grounding tool. Journaling is a means of sharing your innermost thoughts, desires, fears and longings with complete trust that they remain completely private.

The best time to journal is usually first thing in the

morning or last thing at night. Find some time where you can sit for a while, uninterrupted and at peace. Perhaps it may be useful to do this after meditation or even a yoga session. With a favourite notebook and pen, write in a state of flow, allowing things to express themselves through you and to you.

If you are feeling stuck for something to write about, it is always useful to list things you are grateful for. This can help shift your focus from stress and negativity to positivity and contentment. Over time, journaling will allow you the opportunity to reflect, to look back at the different experiences, reactions and even versions of yourself as you continue to grow.

6. Mindful Yoga

Yoga, the ancient Indian practice combines the flexibility of physical postures, breathing exercises, and meditation. Practised correctly it encourages you to focus on your body and your breath. Yoga in and of itself is really just a simple range of stretching exercises and postures.

However, when done purposefully with focus on intention, of watching each breath as we hold each of the postures, paying close attention to how our body feels and reacts as we work through each helps us be more mindful and more aware of our body. In turn we learn trust in our own insights and abilities.

7. Connecting with Nature

Spending time in nature can have a powerful grounding effect. Whether it's a walk in the park, a hike in the woods, or simply sitting in a garden, nature provides an environment that naturally nurtures mindfulness and tranquillity.

Taking some time out of each day to spend in the outdoors, whether it's a quiet stroll in your own backyard or garden, or a longer walk through the woods or through a park, when we spend time in nature, our mind and body natural tunes to a more calming more contented feeling. This is especially true of we are purposeful and mindful when we are in our surroundings, ensuring that we pay attention to our immediate environment, and to our body's responses.

Spending time in nature, not only helps us build an awareness of how connected we are to the greater physical world, but also helps us be more aware and hopefully learn to appreciate the wonder of the world we live in.

Questions for self-reflection
1. How do you typically react when faced with unexpected challenges, and how can mindfulness techniques aid in your response?
2. Which grounding techniques resonate most with you, and why?

STAYING GROUNDED WITH MINDFUL AWARENESS

Any of these techniques when practiced regularly can help you stay grounded amidst the busy chaos that is everyday life. But remember, the goal is never to ignore or avoid the chaos, but instead to develop a centred calmness that will help you to navigate through life's most demanding moments. It is about finding stillness within chaos, peace within turmoil, and anchoring ourselves in the present, even as the world around us revolves in constant motion. This practice of being mindful can lead the way to a deeper experience of joy and contentment, irrespective of the challenges life presents.

By practicing mindful awareness, we can rediscover the joy in ordinary moments and maintain our balance even amidst chaos. This journey requires patience and practice, but the rewards are immense— a deeper, more sustained sense of joy and fulfilment that permeates every aspect of our lives.

Through mindful awareness, we learn to appreciate the simple pleasures that often go unnoticed, finding joy in the warmth of a morning sunrise, the laughter of loved ones, or the gentle touch of a cool breeze. By directing our attention to the present moment, we awaken to the richness of life and discover that joy can be found in the most ordinary experiences.

Mindful awareness also helps us let go of distractions and worries, allowing us to fully engage with the present and experience a deeper sense of contentment and fulfilment. In embracing the practice of mindful awareness, we embrace a greater capacity to savour the precious moments of our lives and find joy in the ordinary.

Questions for self-reflection
1. Can you identify moments in your day when you feel most disconnected from the present? How might integrating mindfulness practices into these times benefit you?
2. How does your physical environment impact your

ability to stay grounded, and what changes could you make to support a more mindful space?

We remind ourselves that joy is not limited to grand achievements or extraordinary events. It can be found in the ordinary, in the everyday routines that shape our lives. By changing our perspectives and attuning our senses, we can begin to recognise the inherent beauty and joy that surrounds us.

May we approach each day with open hearts and fresh eyes, ready to embrace the beauty and joy that lie in the simplest of moments.

Questions for self-reflection
1. What challenges do you foresee in maintaining a consistent mindfulness practice, and how can you overcome them?
2. How has your perception of the world changed as you've delved deeper into the principles of mindfulness and grounded presence?

3
NATURE'S BEAUTY

In every walk with nature, one receives far more than he seeks.

— JOHN MUIR

Nature offers us a sanctuary from the rush of everyday life, a place where we can reconnect, find peace, and often rediscover our capacity for joy. Nature's beauty and its tranquillity has the power to help soothe our minds, heal our hearts, and inspire our souls. This chapter examines the joy that comes from appreciating nature's beauty, and explores the different ways in which we can deepen our connection with the natural world around us.

ENGAGING THE SENSES TO TRULY APPRECIATE OUR SURROUNDINGS

We often experience nature visually. We marvel at the vibrant colours of a sunset or pause in awe at the grandeur of a mountain range. However, nature has a lot more to offer when we take the time to engage in it with all of our senses.

Tuning in to nature by listening closely to the sounds, or becoming aware of the different scents of nature or feeling the gentle winds and breezes can enhance our connection with the environment. As we learn to become more aware of our surroundings, and take time to immerse ourselves wholly in nature, tuning in with all of our senses we participate in a more enveloping experience. We learn to let go of our detached notion of self and begin to appreciate the wholeness of our being as a part of nature. This in turn helps us truly appreciate all of nature's beauty.

Questions for self-reflection
1. Which sensory experiences tend to resonate with you the most when immersed in nature, and why do you think that is?
2. How has a lack of sensory engagement affected your past experiences in natural settings?

1. Sight – Seeing Nature with Fresh Eyes

Sight is often our first point of engagement with the natural world. From panoramic landscapes to minute details like dewdrops on a leaf, nature presents an endless array of visuals upon which we can feast our eyes.

When you are out and about in nature, try to pay attention to colours, patterns, and movements around you. Notice how many graduations and shades of green there may be in a grassy patch or in the leaves of the trees. As you notice how the light falls, you might observe how the shadows play off and over each leaf layer as they create shadow patterns upon the lower canopy. Try to notice the intricate details that are often so easy to overlook, especially when we are in a rush to get through the day — the different shapes of the leaves, the colours of the leaf's veins, the texture of tree bark, the pattern on a butterfly's wings, even the shimmery dance of sunlight on water.

In short, when you are out and about (in nature), whether it is a stroll around the local park or simply a walk around your neighbourhood take your time and observe the larger picture surrounding you. As you take in the larger landscapes, take notice of the minute intricacies too. Tiny details that you might normally miss – a spider's web, a patient bee, perhaps even a lady bug or a flower pushing up through the sidewalk. There is a lot to be seen and to be appreciated if we take some time to notice the little things around us.

2. Sound: Listening to Nature's Symphony

If you live in the city, you may be forgiven if you are constantly trying to tune out of the busy sounds from the environment and choose to keep your ears covered in noise-cancelling headphones. Nature, however is full of sounds that we often take for granted, the rhythmic rustle of leaves, the resonant call of a distant bird. Sounds in nature are often subtle and gentle, but present all the same

When you are spending time in nature, take some time to close your eyes and focus on the sounds that you can hear.

When we can attune ourselves to nature's orchestra, we begin to enter a state of deeper awareness and relaxation. Every day, take a moment to listen to the rhythm of the rain, or the wind whispering through the trees, the chorus of birds at dawn or dusk. And even if you cannot truly tune out the noises of a busy city, try and incorporate what you can hear into your awareness and realisation of the power of your hearing. The sounds of cars along the road, the shrill call of a siren, and then sudden quiet - all of them are part and parcel of this beautiful world we live in.

The magic of nature's sounds reminds us that we are all a part of a larger scheme in the natural world. Even when we sit in still silence and simply contemplate the sounds around us, we are in effect a participant in the performance of the natural world.

https://earth.fm is an excellent resource of nature's sounds online.

3. Smell: Inhaling Nature's Fragrances

Our sense of smell is closely linked to memory and emotion, making it an immensely powerful way to connect with the natural environment. The natural world is full of different aromas, each unique in its own way. From the fresh scent of pine trees or eucalyptus, the sweet fragrance of flowers, to the earthy smell of a forest after rain, these smells can evoke feelings of peace, joy, and a sense of being grounded.

Our olfactory sense is usually one of our least developed senses as we rely mainly on our sense of sight and sound. Still, smells are an extremely evocative way to remind ourselves of experiences past and to help us create new memories. To be able to appreciate the salty-sweet smell of the seaside air, or the tangy must of wild garlic in spring time, our sense of smell although so often under-rated and under-utilised is one of the most powerful of our senses in nature.

The earthy smell of the river, for me brings back childhood memories as we tramped and played right at the river mouth just where it flowed into the sea. Similarly one of my favourite smells is petrichor, that earthy scent of when rain hits the earth, for some reason it calms me and reminds me of renewal and new beginnings.

4. Touch: Feeling Nature's Textures

Our ability to form a physical connection with nature can help us become more grounded in the space that we occupy for the moment. Physically connecting to nature, running our fingers over grass, examining the rough bark of a tree or appreciating the smooth surface of a river stone, the textures in nature are as diverse as they are interesting.

Feel the coolness of water in a stream and the warmth of sand under your feet, or the subtle breeze on your skin. These tactile experiences can bring us closer to nature, offering comfort, curiosity, and a sense of harmony.

5. Taste: Savouring Nature's Flavours

Although taste is not often a sense we associate with the exploration of nature and the outdoors, occasionally we are gifted with the opportunity to taste while we are out in the 'wild'. We do need to be careful about what we taste in nature. We need to be certain that the wild berries we pick or the fruit we pluck off the tree are safe and edible.

Taste the sweet tanginess of a berry picked straight from a bush, the freshness of mint leaves, or the unique flavour of edible flowers. Always ensure that what you're tasting is safe and edible – guided foraging trips can be a wonderful way to safely explore this aspect.

Engaging in all of our senses when we are out in nature allows us to immerse ourselves in fully, helping us foster a deeper understanding and appreciation of our environment. This awareness will make our encounters with nature more meaningful and heartfelt, elevating ordinary moments into extraordinary ones, and filling our hearts with joy and wonder. The next time you find yourself in the great outdoors, take a moment to pause, engage all your senses, and savour all that nature has to offer you. Beyond just enjoying being physically in the outdoors, immersing yourself in nature is known to have a therapeutic effect.

CONNECTING WITH NATURE AND ITS HEALING POWER

Our connection to nature is as ancient as humanity itself. From early ancestors who relied upon the natural world for sustenance and shelter, to modern humans who now seek solace and rejuvenation in the great outdoors, nature has been an integral part of our existence.

THE HUMAN-NATURE CONNECTION

The human affinity for nature, 'biophilia[1]' first coined by biologist E.O. Wilson, refers to our inherent love of nature. It refers to our intuitive and natural need to connect with the natural world. Whether it is the tranquillity of a forest, the rhythmic sound of ocean waves, or the breath-taking view from a mountaintop, nature has a way of invoking a sense of peace and well-being.

Modern research supports this human-nature[2] bond. Numerous studies[3] have found that exposure to nature reduces stress, anxiety, and depression, while enhancing mood, focus, and overall happiness. One influential study[4] found that even just viewing images of nature can decrease stress levels and promote recovery from mental fatigue.

These positive effects can be attributed to several factors. Nature provides a respite from the constant stimuli of the urban environment, offering a serene space where our minds can relax and recharge. It encourages physical activity and social interaction, both known for their mood-enhancing benefits. Moreover, natural environments stimulate our senses in a gentle way, fostering mindfulness and a deeper connection to the world around us.

Questions for self-reflection
1. How do moments in nature influence your overall outlook on life and the bigger picture?
2. When was the last time nature made you feel truly humbled, and why?

NATURE'S HEALING POWER

The concept of 'forest bathing,' or shinrin-yoku in Japanese, has gained popularity, not just in Japan but also all around the world for its positive effects on psychology and physiology.[5] This practice involves immersing oneself in a forest environment and mindfully engaging with the surroundings through all five senses. Research on forest bathing has shown that it can boost immune function, reduce blood pressure, improve sleep, even alleviate symptoms of depression.

However, you do not need a forest to connect with nature and harness its healing power. If you do have easy access to a nature park, make full use of it. However, if you live in a more urban environment, then there are some other accessible ways to foster your connection with the natural world.

Questions for self-reflection
1. How can you incorporate nature's healing properties into your daily routines or rituals?
2. Which natural settings or practices make you feel most rejuvenated?

1. Nature Walks

Regular walks in nature, whether in a local park, by a lake, or in the woods, can have a positive impact on your well-being. Pay attention to the sights – the different shades of green, the various textures of the bark on tree trunks; the sounds of nature – different bird songs, rustling leaves, and the scents and smells around you. Take your time and immerse yourself in nature let its tranquillity wash over you.

Let go of your worries and concerns for a while and focus on simply being where you are.

The Great Dell is a park that is fairly local to me. However, it is actually smack right in the middle of a city. Every time I get there early enough, before the rush of commuter traffic, there is a silence and stillness that permeates through the park accentuated by birds singing, the rustling of leaves. There are a great many varied trees, but among my favourite is a Californian redwood, that seems out of place in an English city park, yet feels like it cannot be anywhere else. Whenever I am in the presence of that redwood, I take some time out to lay my hands on its wonderfully coloured, soft textured bark, so different from any of the other trees nearby. I feel a great appreciation for nature, for the various trees and plants and the range of animals that call the Great Dell home.

Questions for self-reflection
1. How does the pace and intent of your walk in nature influence the experiences and feelings you derive from it?
2. What sounds, sights, or sensations do you anticipate or hope for before embarking on a nature walk?

2. Gardening

Gardening is another therapeutic activity that will bring you in touch with nature and also instil a sense of responsibility and care for other living things. It is deeply satisfying to watch plants grow and thrive under your care. Getting your hands dirty in the soil also actually increases different organic acids and serotonin (happy brain chemical) levels in the body. This has been attributed to a specific bacterium that lives naturally in the soil, *Mycobacterium vaccae*, with researchers concluding that human contact and exposure to soil resulted in positive psychological and physiological changes.[6]

Questions for self-reflection
1. How does the act of nurturing a plant from seed to bloom make you feel about growth and life cycles?
2. What unexpected lessons have you learned from spending time gardening or caring for plants?

3. Outdoor Meditation

Meditation is often something we strive to practise in a quiet and silent environment. We believe that the less distracting an environment, the easier it is to meditate. In many ways, this is true. However, meditating in the great outdoors, might allow us to watch our thoughts and accept the ebb and flow of emotions and wandering minds as we 'lose' ourselves for a moment.

Sit under a tree, on a beach, or in your garden, and focus on the natural sounds and sensations around you. Instead of the traditional meditative practise of 'emptying your mind' perhaps when you are practising meditation outdoors, simply allow each and everyone of nature's beauties to reveal themselves in turn – the light filtering through leaves and branches, sounds of birds calling out to each other, footsteps of others enjoying and appreciating the same space. An outdoor meditation might even help deepen your meditation practice while enhancing your connection with nature.

Questions for self-reflection
1. How does meditating outdoors differ from indoor sessions for you in terms of depth and connection?
2. What elements of nature most enhance or distract from your meditation experience, and why?

4. Wildlife Observation

If you have access to a space where wild animals visit, spend time observing them in their natural habitats. If you're near a river, look out for visiting ducks and geese, even swans over the warmer seasons. Look in to the water at the fishes, insets and other wildlife that live on the water's edge. If you're near the hills, look out for deer, squirrels, even rabbits and moles.

If you're blessed with a large or even a small garden, look out for visiting bees and butterflies, ladybirds. Taking time, even if it is just a couple of minutes a day to observe and notice the life that surrounds us will help us cultivate patience, awe, and a deeper appreciation for the complexity and beauty of life in all its myriad forms.

Questions for self-reflection
1. How does observing wildlife behaviors and interactions shift your perspective on your own life and its complexities?
2. What wildlife moments have provided you with the deepest sense of wonder?

5. Bring Nature Indoors

If your access to outdoor spaces is limited, try and bring nature indoors. Houseplants, nature sounds, landscape photographs and images all contribute to creating a calmer environment and helps us foster a sense of connection to the natural world.

Ultimately connecting with nature is more than just a leisure activity—it is a fundamental aspect of well-being, offering a source of peace, healing, and joy. As we work to deepen our bond with nature, we not only improve our physical and mental health, but we also develop a greater appreciation and fascination for the beauty and intricacy of the world we inhabit. This in turn enriches our lives and fosters a path towards a more joyful and fulfilled existence.

> *Questions for self-reflection*
> 1. How does the introduction of natural elements indoors shift the energy and mood of your space?
> 2. Which nature-inspired items or practices indoors bring you the greatest sense of peace?

FINDING JOY IN THE CHANGING SEASONS: AN EXPLORATION

Each season paints a unique picture, from the vibrant colours of fall and the serene stillness of winter, to the rebirth in spring and the abundance of summer. These changes not only provide a feast for the eyes but also serve as a reminder of life's cyclical nature and the beauty of impermanence.

Take time to observe and revel in these changes. Watch the leaves turn from green to shades of gold, red, and brown in the fall. Witness the snow transforming the landscape into a white wonderland in winter. Feel the renewed energy in spring as flowers bloom and trees come alive. And enjoy the lush greenery and vibrant life that summer brings.

Natural wonders such as rainbows, sunsets, starry nights, and the rhythm of the ocean can fill us with awe and joy. These experiences provide moments of transcendence, reminding us of the grandeur of the universe and our place within it.

Nature, with its ever-changing colours, rhythms, and sounds, provides us with an ongoing spectacle of beauty and awe. The shifting of seasons and the stunning natural wonders that punctuate our planet offer countless opportunities to encounter joy and wonderment. This section delves into the delights these changes can bring and how they can enrich our appreciation of the world around us.

REVELLING IN THE CHANGING SEASONS

The changing seasons, with their distinct character and charm, provide a sensory feast and a fresh perspective of the natural world. Each season represents a different stage in the cycle of life, reflecting themes of birth, growth, decay, and rest. This serves as a powerful metaphor for our own lives and the beauty of constant change.

Spring is a time of rebirth and renewal. It often feels magical as early bulbs creep out from under frosty ground. Plants prepare to burst into life the moment the temperature rises even slightly and the many insects and animals that have been hibernating through the cold awaken from their winter slumber. Closely observing and participating in this explosion of life, from appreciating blossoming flowers to listening closely to chirping birds, can bring immense joy and a sense of hope in the renewal of life.

Summer with its long days and abundant activity of life, invites us to spend time outdoors, soaking up the sun, and enjoying nature at its full bloom. Trees that are a full of vibrant leaves, gardens brimming with flowers and fruits. The warm weather and the vibrant colours naturally evokes feelings of happiness and vitality.

Autumn is nature's grand finale, as it adorns the landscape in rich hues of red, orange, and gold. This change can be a reminder of the beauty in transitions and the inescapable cycle of life and death. There is a certain pleasure in walking through crisp autumn leaves, breathing in the earthy scents, and feeling the gentle chill in the air. There's a slowing down in the general pace of life in nature as everything starts preparing to wind down.

Winter with its bare trees and blanketed landscapes, may seem devoid of life, but it offers its own stark beauty. It brings a peaceful silence, an invitation to slow down, reflect, and appreciate the restful, quiet phase of nature. It is a time for resting and resetting. An opportunity to take things slow and easy, and to be kinder and gentler to ourselves.

Questions for self-reflection
1. How does each season resonate differently with you in terms of emotions, memories, and sensations?
2. How can you harness the unique attributes of each season to enrich your mindfulness practices?

MARVELLING AT NATURAL WONDERS

Apart from the cyclical seasonal changes, nature herself presents us with awe-inspiring wonders that captivate our senses and fill us with joy. Observing an early morning radiant sunrise or being present as the sun sets in to the far horizon, sleeping under the boundless night sky adorned with stars, or watching a rainbow arch across the sky after a rain shower, can be deeply moving experiences.

These moments are not just visually stunning but are reminders of the grandeur and intricacy of our universe. They evoke from us a sense of awe — a reminder of the gift of our life and our being present in the greater scheme of the world. Research[7] has shown that the awe that we experience can increase happiness, reduce stress, and even inspire creativity and a sense of connectedness.

Here are some ways to further deepen your appreciation of these natural wonders:

1. Nature Photography

Taking pictures of the natural world can be a joyful practice. Whether you spontaneously capture moments on your mobile phone camera or wait for the perfect moment on your professional SLR, taking photographs helps us to see details we might have missed. On the hunt for natures visuals also encourages us to seek out the beauty in every corner of nature.

2. Nature Journaling

Writing about experiences in nature, the changing seasons, and the wonders you observe can also help to enhance your appreciation and help you connect more deeply with each of these experiences.

Remember these notes need not be perfect and they can take any written form that you may be inspired to write, from poetry to entire articles. The idea is to simply express in writing, your experience, thoughts and emotions that arise during your time in nature.

3. Shared Experiences

Sharing these moments with others can enhance our joy. Whether it's a walk through a forest ablaze with autumn colours or stargazing on a clear night, shared experiences can foster deeper connections with both nature and with each other.

Finding joy in the changing seasons and natural wonders is about more than just appreciating beautiful scenery. It is about connecting with the rhythms of life, embracing change, and marvelling at the vastness and intricacies of our world and the greater universe. By immersing ourselves in these experiences, we can cultivate a deep sense of joy, wonder, and gratitude for the world around us.

Questions for self-reflection
1. How do awe-inspiring moments in nature shape your perceptions of beauty and grandeur in the world?
2. Which natural wonders have left the deepest impression on you, and why?

Connecting with nature is more than just a leisure activity—it's a fundamental aspect of well-being, offering a source of peace, healing, and joy. As we deepen our bond with nature, we not only improve our physical and mental health, but we also develop a greater appreciation for the beauty and intricacy of the world we inhabit. This enriches our lives and fosters a path towards a more joyful and fulfilled existence.

By building a deeper connection and appreciation of nature, we can tap into a rich source of joy and tranquility. Nature serves as a mirror, reflecting back to us our own inherent beauty and the rhythm of life that pulses within us. It gently nudges us to slow down, to appreciate the moment, and to discover joy in our surroundings, thereby enriching our journey toward joyful living.

4
EVERYDAY MOMENTS: MAKING THE ORDINARY EXTRAORDINARY

Joy does not simply happen to us. We have to choose joy and keep choosing it every day.

— HENRI J.M. NOUWEN

In our busy, demanding lives, we rush through our daily routines often on auto-pilot with little care or thought. Our aim often focussed entirely on juggling and getting through each day with as little disruption or distraction as possible. Yet, in doing so, we overlook a wealth of joy and fulfilment that can be found in the simplicity and familiarity of our everyday lives.

This chapter invites you to pause, take a breath, and ease into the art of savouring the ordinary moments. By embracing the beauty in our routines, practicing mindful eating, and creating meaningful rituals, we can infuse in to our daily lives and emerge once again with a profound sense of joy and contentment.

RECOGNIZING AND EMBRACING THE BEAUTY IN EVERYDAY ROUTINES

The boring and routine tasks of our everyday lives are often lumped together as tedious obligations that take our time away from what we perceive might be more exciting and more fulfilling activities. However, when we change our perception and approach them with a sense of presence and mindfulness, these tasks can become an abundant source of joy and beauty. This concept may sound foreign or counterintuitive, but over time and with practice, we can find unexpected joy in the ordinary tasks that fill our days.

Firstly, to change our relationship with everyday routines, we must recognise their inherent value. Our daily routines, whether they involve cleaning, cooking, commuting, or even bathing, offer a sense of structure and stability. They are necessary tasks that contribute to our overall well-being and comfort. These are not meaningless activities to rush through, but opportunities to find a moment of calm amidst the chaos of life.

Begin by bringing conscious attention to these tasks. For instance, while washing the dishes, focus on the sensation of warm water running over your hands, the smell of the soap, the clink of dishes as you stack them. Paying attention to the minute details of an activity can turn a mundane chore into a mindful, grounding activity. This is not about finding excitement or novelty in these tasks but about being present and finding contentment in the process.

Next, try to develop a sense of gratitude for these activities. This might seem challenging, particularly if you find these tasks tiresome. However, each task offers something to be grateful for — it could be as simple as the comfort of clean clothes, the nourishment from a home-cooked meal, or the freshness of a clean home. Recognising these benefits can help shift your perspective from viewing these tasks as burdens to seeing them as essential aspects of your well-being.

Finally, find beauty in the rhythm and repetition of these tasks. The world around us often seems fast-paced and chaotic. In contrast, our everyday routines provide a steady rhythm, a reliable pattern that we return to day after day. There's a certain beauty in this predictability, a subtle harmony that offers a sense of stability and grounding.

Embracing the beauty in everyday routines doesn't happen overnight. It takes practice and patience. But as we gradually shift our mindset, we'll find that these moments of washing dishes, sweeping floors, or commuting to work are not just empty spaces to be filled with distractions. They're opportunities for mindfulness, for finding peace in the present moment, for appreciating the simple and ordinary aspects of our lives. By recognising and embracing this, we open ourselves to a greater sense of contentment and joy in our daily lives.

Questions for self-reflection
1. When have you felt a deep sense of satisfaction or peace in a seemingly mundane task? What were you doing?
2. How can you shift your perspective to view a daily chore you currently dislike as an opportunity for mindfulness and grounding?

MINDFUL EATING AND SAVOURING THE FLAVOURS OF LIFE

Food – diet and eating is such a large part of our lives. Whether we are diet watchers or snack grabbers, whether we truly enjoy food or have a love-hate relationship with it, food is an essential part of our daily lives. Sadly though, the joy of a shared meal and the appreciation of a delicious home-cooked meal, is no longer as appreciated or as sacred as it used to be.

In our hurried lives, meals are often scoffed down in a hurry, in front of screens, or on the go. Busy mums and children often eat snacks, even meals in the car while transitioning from school to activity to home. Who among us hasn't shoved down a sandwich in front of our work computer? The detached way that we eat leads to a disconnection, not only from the people with whom we can and should share our meals but also from the food that we eat and the process of eating itself. Mindful eating invites us to slow down and fully engage with our meals, turning them into a source of pleasure and an opportunity to increase our self-awareness.

Mindful eating[1] is about paying full attention to the *experience* of eating and drinking. It involves noticing the colours, smells, textures, flavours, temperatures, and even the sounds of our food. It is about learning to make choices that support our health and well-being, and becoming aware of physical hunger and cues of satiation to guide our decisions as to when and how much we need or want to eat. Here are some strategies to practice mindful eating.

. . .

1. Remove distractions

How often do we plonk ourselves down in front of television with a plate of food on our laps, focussed entirely on the screen in front of us? When we multi-task we are no longer paying attention or being mindful about what we are doing. In this case, when we eat in front of the television, we are certainly not paying attention to the food we are eating nor are we able to appreciate it.

To eat more mindfully, find a quiet place to eat without distractions. Turn off the television, put away the mobile phones and shut down the computers. These only take away from the mindful eating experience by splitting your focus. Ideally, eat at a dinner table and at family meal times, try to make time for everyone to eat together.

2. Engage with all your senses

Before you begin eating, take a moment to appreciate the visual appeal of your food — its colours, its appearance and finish even its aroma. As you eat, pay attention to the texture and taste of each bite. Notice the crunch of a crisp apple, the tanginess of yogurt, the warmth of a freshly baked bread.

Eating is an activity that calls into use several of our senses simultaneously. To be able to enjoy the food we eat, it is good to be aware, not just of how the food is presented, but also of the smells, tastes, texture and aromas.

3. Savour your food — eat slowly

We often eat far too quickly, so much so that we do not really taste nor appreciate our food. An important way to begin enjoying food is to consciously make yourself eat more slowly — take smaller bites and chew more slowly and thoroughly. This will help you to fully experience the flavours, textures and aroma of your meal.

4. Check-in with yourself

When we are in a hurry, and we just chow down our food, we pay little attention to how much we are actually eating. Often, we are more likely to overeat[2] when we do not pay attention to what we are eating.

Regularly pause throughout the meal to assess your hunger and fullness levels. This can help you avoid overeating and ensure that you are more in tune with your body's food intake needs.

5. Express gratitude

Take a moment to express gratitude for your meal, considering all the effort that went into producing, transporting, preparing, and serving the food on your plate. This will heighten your appreciation of the meal.

While many of us are familiar with saying grace before meal times, some cultures, the Japanese for instance, say a simple itadakimasu (translated to 'I humbly receive') which adds a value of gratitude and appreciation in accepting and enjoying the food and the experience of eating.

6. Make eating a ritual

It is worth creating a calm and enjoyable eating environment. This might mean setting the table nicely, even if you're eating alone, lighting a candle, or even playing some soft background music. Ritualising the mealtime can make it a more cherished and mindful part of your day. It allows you to slow down, to enjoy the meal and the environment in which you eat and to take your time to eat slowly and mindfully.

Practicing mindful eating can transform our relationship with food. It not only enhances our enjoyment and appreciation of meals but also allows us to be more in tune with our bodies and its needs. By making the act of eating a more deliberate and mindful practice, we can truly savour the flavours of life, turning each meal into a moment of joy and gratitude.

Questions for self-reflection
1. Think about your last meal. Were you fully present, or were distractions pulling you away from truly enjoying it?
2. How might creating a dedicated environment for eating, free from screens or work, change your relationship with food?

CREATING RITUALS TO ENHANCE DAILY EXPERIENCES

Rituals, distinct from routines, are intentional actions performed with a sense of purpose and presence. They offer a means of expressing and connecting with our personal values, creating moments of meaning in our everyday lives. By transforming simple daily activities into cherished rituals, we can bring a heightened sense of awareness, enjoyment, and fulfilment to our days.

Rituals can be as simple or as complex as you wish, but

they share a few common characteristics. They are intentional, meaning that they're done with a purpose in mind, and mindful, meaning they involve a focus on the present moment. They often have a repetitive nature, carried out at the same time every day perhaps, establishing a sense of familiarity and comfort. More importantly, they are often imbued with a sense of significance, beyond the immediate task at hand.

One of my own daily rituals involves yoga every morning at six, however while the practise of yoga at that time has become habitual, the ritual before I start yoga, involves lighting a candle and the offering of a refreshed cup of water at the small Buddhist altar in my home. While this may seem to be a religious ritual, the ritual you may choose to practise does not have to be; it simply has to be something you consciously enjoy, and in doing it, it puts you into a calm and peaceful frame of mind.

Here are some suggestions of how to create rituals that can enhance your daily experiences.

1. Identify meaningful activities

Begin by identifying daily activities that bring you joy, comfort, or a sense of well-being. This could be anything from enjoying a cup of coffee in the morning, taking a midday walk, or winding down in the evening with a good book. The key is to choose activities that resonate with you. Any meaningful activity when repeated consistently and repeatedly becomes a ritual.

· · ·

2. Set an intention

Once you have chosen an activity, set an intention for your ritual. This could be to create a sense of calm, to express gratitude, or simply to savour a moment of joy. This intention is what elevates the activity from a routine to a ritual.

3. Cultivate mindfulness

As you perform your ritual, bring your full attention to the activity. Notice the sights, sounds, smells, and sensations involved. If your mind wanders, gently bring it back to the present moment. This mindfulness deepens the experience and heightens your sense of connection and enjoyment.

4. Add personal touches

Incorporate elements that make the ritual uniquely yours. This could be setting the ambiance with candles or music, using a special cup for your morning coffee, or saying a short gratitude prayer before your meal. These conscious choices add greater intention and purpose to the ritual, helping to make it a more cherished part of your day.

5. Maintain consistency

Rituals derive their power from repetition. The familiarity and predictability of performing the same actions in the same way provide a sense of comfort and grounding. Aim to perform your rituals consistently, but remember that the goal is not perfection. If you miss a day, simply return to the ritual the next day without self-judgment.

Questions for self-reflection
1. What's one daily activity that you believe could become a cherished ritual with a bit more intention?
2. How do you personalise or add significance to the routines in your life, turning them into more meaningful rituals?

Creating rituals offer us an opportunity to infuse our daily experiences with a greater sense of purpose, joy, and fulfilment. They provide anchors of stability in our often chaotic lives, moments of mindfulness in our busy days. They are also a means of honouring our personal values as part of our everyday actions. By creating rituals that resonate and align with our core values, we enhance our daily experiences and create a life filled with more joy and meaning.

Savouring everyday moments is an invitation to slow down and reconnect with the present moment. By finding beauty in our routines, enjoying our meals mindfully, and establishing purposeful rituals, we can infuse joy, peace, and gratitude into our daily lives. Through these practices, we begin to transform the ordinary into the extraordinary and begin to see the beauty in, and appreciate the miracle of everyday life.

5
MEANINGFUL CONNECTIONS: THE JOY IN TOGETHERNESS

Joy is not in things; it is in us.

— RICHARD WAGNER

We are all inherently social beings, even if some of us may sometimes prefer our own company (introverts) while others love the buzz of social gatherings. Our relationships and connections with others play a vital role in our overall well-being and happiness.

When we know that we are able to call upon and rely on family and friends, we become more confident in our outlook on life — we know that 'someone has our back'. Similarly, when we are willing to be present and available for our friends and family to call upon, we feel that we are able to contribute to their well-being, and we accept that we play a valued and trusted role in their lives.

In this chapter, we examine the art of cultivating meaningful connections. We will explore the joy and fulfilment derived from building and nurturing relationships, expressing gratitude and kindness to others, and sharing joyous experiences with others.

> *Questions for self-reflection*
> 1. How has your understanding of human connection evolved over time?
> 2. When faced with disagreements in relationships, how do you usually react and why?

FINDING JOY IN RELATIONSHIPS AND HUMAN CONNECTION

Human connection is a vital part of our existence. We thrive on interaction, collaboration, and the mutual sharing of experiences and emotions. Healthy relationships foster a sense of belonging and provide us with emotional support, contributing to our overall happiness and well-being. Research[1] has shown that connecting[2] with others not only improves our health but helps to increase our life span by about 50%.

A key to building and nurturing relationships is the ability to listen empathetically. This means, for example, that instead of just asking 'How are you?' and expecting a vague 'All, good' or 'Fine' in response, when we ask how someone is, we open ourselves up to consciously wanting to know how that person really is. It means being prepared to listen to the woes of the day, or join in joyous celebration of an achievement or success. It means that when we ask about how someone is, we are genuinely prepared to pay attention and to listen.

We need to actively listen with the intent of understanding another's thoughts, feelings, and perspectives without rushing to judge or offer unsolicited advice. When people genuinely feel heard and understood, trust and intimacy creates a stronger bond between the people in that relationship. Feeling connected and being connected, even if it is only through a conversation reminds us that we are not alone.

Open and honest communication is crucial in maintaining and strengthening relationships. This involves expressing your thoughts and feelings in a respectful and considerate manner, as well as being open to feedback and criticism. It is about having the courage to voice our own needs without being worried about being judged. It is also about the openness of trying to understand and to help meet the needs and requirements that others may have. Clear and compassionate communication can prevent misunderstandings, resolve conflicts, and deepen the connection between individuals.

Mutual respect and appreciation is of course a given when we are building and nurturing relationships with others. When we respect and appreciate another, we acknowledge the individuality of the other person. We respect their rights, choices, and opinions, even when they are different from our own. It also means appreciating them wholly for who they are, recognising their qualities, both good and bad, and expressing this appreciation openly.

When people feel respected and appreciated, they learn to know and recognise the value within themselves and all they contribute. They become more open to also looking for and focussing on the positive traits of the people with whom they interact. It helps them to reciprocate these feelings and recognition in others, helping to create a positive and more secure, valued and satisfying relationship.

Relationships cannot function without the investment of time and effort. Much like plants, relationships between friends need regular attention and care to grow and flourish. While this may be as simple as sending a brief 'How have you been?' to an old friend who lives far away, for others, it may require more purposeful organising, to meet up for coffee or join an exercise class together.

Spending quality time together, participating in shared activities, and regularly checking in with each other helps remind us that we are not alone in this journey through life. It helps us remember that there are people we can call upon in our time of need and a ready crowd to have fun and celebrate with us, our successes. The time and effort invested in these relationships will yield strong emotional connections and a great sense of being connected to a wider support group, while giving us satisfaction and joy.

Although distance often seems like an unsurmountable challenge to maintaining close relationships, with the tools of technology, communicating and maintaining contact is no longer the challenge it used to be.

We no longer have to rely on weeks-long snail-mail letters, or pricey phone cards to make international calls. With the advent of online and mobile applications such as WhatsApp, various messengers, and even online conferencing and video chat software, getting in touch and staying in touch is straightforward, cheap and easy.

While the ease of digital communication helps ensure that we can stay in touch, even share via video important live moments in our life. On top of that, the ability to participate in various activities — play online games, watch movies, even share a book simultaneously has been made possible through technology. While being physically present may not always be easy, with technology, we are far more connected now than we ever used to be.

In essence, nurturing relationships, enjoying getting to know people and finding joy in human connection isn't always about grand gestures. It's about the simple, consistent acts of love, understanding, and care we show to the people in our lives. It is about finding joy in their company, sharing experiences, being honest about our feelings and emotions, and growing together in mutual respect and understanding. By consciously nurturing our connections with the people in our lives and making new connections too, we open our lives to a greater depth of joy, fulfilment, and emotional well-being.

Questions for self-reflection
1. What actions can you take to deepen the connections in your current relationships?
2. Are there any relationships in your life that may need reevaluation or renewed effort?

EXPRESSING APPRECIATION AND KINDNESS TO OTHERS

'Thank you' 'I appreciate you' 'So grateful for you' expressing appreciation, gratitude and kindness are powerful tools that can transform our lives and the lives of those around us. They help to strengthen our relationships, boost our own happiness and well-being, and create a positive ripple effect in our communities.

Appreciation is the acknowledgment of the value, significance, or magnitude of people and things. It involves recognising and affirming the good qualities, values or the actions of others. Expressing appreciation help to make people feel seen and valued, while strengthening the emotional bonds between individuals. In relationships, expressing appreciation can foster a greater sense of intimacy and mutual respect. It helps to remind people of their worth and their positive impact on our lives.

Showing appreciation can take many forms. It can be as simple as expressing it verbally, "I appreciate your help," or it can be shown through actions, such as a warm smile, a heartfelt note, or a thoughtful gift. The key is sincerity – your appreciation must be genuine and heartfelt to have the most significant impact.

Meanwhile, kindness represents the actions we take to show consideration, generosity, and care towards others. Kindness is not just about being nice — it is about recognising another person's needs and meeting them in some way that has meaningful positive impact on their life.

Expressing kindness can be as simple as offering a compliment, lending a helping hand, or sharing a warm smile. These acts of kindness not only bring happiness to the other person but it can also help boost our own mood. When we have done a good deed, we naturally get a lift of serotonin and dopamine in our brains,[3] which make us feel good. While more substantial acts of kindness might involve volunteering your time to a cause you care about or going out of your way to help someone in need, even simple acts of kindness, a smile, a warm hug can bring positive responses,

Remember, the act of expressing appreciation, gratitude, and kindness should not be done with the expectation of getting something in return. These expressions are most powerful when they are selfless and come from the heart. They can create a positive feedback loop of joy and satisfaction that not only enhances your life but also radiates out to those around you, contributing to a more compassionate and joyful world.

In essence, by consciously incorporating expressions of appreciation, gratitude, and kindness into our daily interactions, we can deepen our connections with others, amplify our own feelings of joy and satisfaction, and contribute to a kinder, more loving world.

Questions for self-reflection
1. How do acts of kindness towards others affect your own well-being?
2. Can you think of a time when you missed the opportunity to express appreciation? How might you handle a similar situation in the future?

MOMENTS OF JOY THROUGH SHARED EXPERIENCES

Almost everyone has a favourite story from a childhood holiday, or a memory from a family occasion, shared experiences serve as powerful bonding tools, creating lasting memories and strengthening relationships among everyone who shared in that experience. Shared memories allow us to connect with others on a deeper level, reinforcing our sense of belonging and mutual understanding. But beyond their social benefits, shared experiences are also powerful sources of personal joy.

When we share an experience with others, whether it is a simple meal or a grand adventure, we are not merely participating in an event. We are co-creating a unique moment, a memory, that will become a part of our collective history. These shared experiences contribute to a shared narrative that deepens our connection to each other. The joy derived from these moments often transcends the immediate pleasure of the activity itself, lingering long after the event has passed.

Creating a shared experiences can be as simple or as elaborate as we want to make it. It might be as straightforward as preparing and sharing a meal with family or friends. The act of working together in the kitchen, the shared laughter and conversation, the enjoyment of the meal – all of these create a collective experience filled with joy.

Alternatively, it might involve more complex activities such as travelling, participating in a community event, or embarking on a shared project. It is not the scale or grandeur of the activity that matters but the quality of the connection and the joy derived from doing something together.

Shared laughter and play are also powerful ways of creating joyous moments. Laughter is a universal language of connection and joy. When we laugh together, barriers crumble, and our hearts open to each other. Similarly, play, often regarded as the domain of children, has equal importance in adult lives. Engaging in playful activities together, be it a board game, a sport, or simply goofing around, releases stress, stimulates creativity, and strengthens our bonds to each other.

Creativity, too, is a fantastic medium for shared experiences. Collaborating on a creative project – such as painting a mural, composing a song, or gardening – allows for self-expression and mutual engagement, cultivating a shared sense of accomplishment and joy.

Mindful sharing of experiences is an essential aspect of deriving joy from shared moments. It involves being fully present and engaged in the activity, being attentive to the sensory experiences, and being open to the emotional connections being formed. It is about truly being with each other in the moment, free from distractions, and savouring the shared experience.

Questions for self-reflection
1. How do shared experiences contribute to your overall sense of happiness and well-being?
2. What's a recent shared experience that surprised you in its ability to bring joy?

In essence, creating moments of joy through shared experiences is about being intentionally present with others. It is about recognising and seizing opportunities for connection and mutual enjoyment and about creating and savouring moments that, woven together, remind each of us that we are but one strand in the larger scheme of our joyous existence. By consciously engaging in shared experiences, we can cultivate deeper relationships that will enrich our lives, help us determine the narratives of kinship and connection, and extend outwards our personal and collective joy.

6

SIMPLE PLEASURES

The greatest joy can be found in the simplest moments, if only we pause to feel.

— UNKNOWN

Our greatest joy almost always comes from the smallest, simplest moments. In the midst of our busy, demanding lives, juggling between work and family demands, striving for achievements and successes, we often overlook the beauty and pleasure of simple things. Embracing simple pleasures – whether it is rediscovering the simple joys of play, indulging in soul-fulfilling hobbies, or celebrating small wins – can bring joy and satisfaction into our lives.

This chapter focuses on how we can choose to focus on joy in the simplest activities and pleasures.

REDISCOVERING THE SIMPLE JOYS OF PLAY AND CREATIVITY

At some point in our journey to adulthood, most of us have relegated the idea of 'play' to the background of our memory. The demands 'and seriousness' of grown-up life leaves little room for playful exploration or for losing ourselves in moments of carefree delight. Yet, as researchers[1] and psychologists[2] have found, play isn't just for children. It's essential for adults too.

Play, in its many forms, has a well-documented positive impact on our wellbeing. It can boost our mood, reduce stress, enhance mental agility, and stimulate creativity. More importantly, play is intrinsically satisfying. It is fun, enjoyable, and brings us joy. When we play, we engage with the world around us in a more interactive and meaningful way. We tap into our imagination, challenge our minds, and often, reconnect with the carefree spirit of our childhood.

Creativity, too, is deeply intertwined with joy. Whether we're painting a picture, writing a story, playing a musical instrument, or even innovating a new recipe, we're engaging in creative expression. Creativity allows us to express ourselves, to give form to our thoughts and emotions, and to view the world from a unique perspective. Like play, creative activities can bring us deeply satisfying joy. These activities can make us lose track of time, immerse us in a state of 'flow', and provide a deep sense of satisfaction.

So how do we integrate play and creativity into our busy, demanding adult lives? One of the ways is to make a conscious effort to dedicate some time each day to playful or creative activities. This does not have to be time-consuming or complicated. It could be as simple as playing a board game with family, doodling in a sketchbook, or experimenting with a new dish in the kitchen.

Joining a local club or community can also provide regular opportunities for play and creativity. It could be a sports team, a book club, a painting class, or a cooking group. These communities not only offer a platform for playful engagement and creative exploration but also provide social interaction, which is another essential aspect of joyful living.

Creating a 'playful' environment at home or work can also foster play and creativity. This might involve having access to playful resources (like games, art supplies, or musical instruments), creating a visually stimulating environment, or simply adopting a more playful mindset towards everyday tasks.

In essence, rediscovering the joy of play and creativity involves breaking away from the notion that they are only for children. By making play and creativity a part of our everyday lives, we can tap into a useful and valuable source of joy, satisfaction, and overall wellbeing. As we unleash our playful spirit and creative potential, we will find ourselves experiencing the world in more joyful and vibrant ways.

Questions for self-reflection
1. When you think back to your childhood, what playful activities made you lose track of time and how might you incorporate those into your adult life?
2. How often do you give yourself permission to be creative without worrying about the end result?

FINDING HAPPINESS IN HOBBIES AND PASSIONS

Hobbies and passions have a unique way of bringing happiness and contentment into our lives. They not only provide an escape from the monotony of our daily routines but also serve as channels for self-expression, personal growth, and even social connection.

Hobbies, in particular, can be a source of immense joy. Be it gardening, knitting, bird watching, baking, dancing, or any activity that sparks our interest - hobbies give us something to look forward to. They provide a sense of purpose and offer an opportunity to immerse ourselves in something we genuinely enjoy. This immersion often leads to a state of 'flow', a mental state in which we are fully absorbed and engaged in an activity, oblivious to the passing of time. This state of flow[3] is linked with increased happiness and satisfaction.

Beyond that, hobbies also stimulate our brains, help develop new skills, and broaden our horizons. They provide a sense of accomplishment when we master a technique or complete a project. Over time, hobbies can also lead to deep personal growth, as we learn to overcome challenges, persist despite setbacks, and express ourselves in new and creative ways.

While hobbies offer a respite from our routines, passions inject our lives with enthusiasm and energy. When we engage in activities we are truly passionate about, it's like lighting a fire within us. Our passions fuel us with motivation, excitement, and a sense of fulfilment. They make us eager to get out of bed in the morning and eager to explore, learn, and grow. Whether our passion lies in music, art, literature, sports, or community service - investing time and energy in these areas can make our lives more rewarding, fulfilled and joyful.

However, identifying and nurturing these passions require self-reflection and conscious effort. We need to take the time to introspect, to understand what activities truly engage us, ignite our curiosity, or provide a sense of purpose. Once we've identified these areas, it is crucial to create space in our lives to pursue these passions. This might involve setting specific goals, scheduling time in our daily routine, or seeking out communities and resources that support our interests.

Ultimately, finding happiness in hobbies and passions is about giving ourselves permission to do what we love. It is about acknowledging that these activities are not just 'extras' or 'luxuries' but essential components of a happy, fulfilling life. By devoting time to our hobbies and passions, we can enrich our lives with joy, purpose, and personal growth.

Questions for self-reflection
1. Is there a hobby you've always wanted to explore but haven't yet, and what's been holding you back?
2. How do you feel when you're deeply engaged in a hobby or passion, and how can you ensure you prioritise that feeling more often?

CELEBRATING EVERY WIN, NO MATTER HOW SMALL

In a world that often seems obsessed with 'big' achievements – large promotions, hefty salary raises, grand ceremonies – it is easy to overlook the value and joy in small victories. Yet, it is these small accomplishments that are the stepping stones that eventually lead us to the larger goals. They are signs of progress and growth, and by celebrating them, we enhance our happiness, self-esteem, and motivation.

Every task we complete, every goal we inch closer to, every new skill we acquire, and every bit of progress we make, deserves recognition. Perhaps you managed to run a little further today, or you finally finished reading that book that's been sitting on your shelf, or you successfully cooked a new recipe. These may seem trivial compared to bigger goals like running a marathon, publishing a book, or becoming a master chef, but they are achievements nonetheless.

Celebrating smaller achievements boosts our mood and reinforces a positive self-image. It creates a sense of satisfaction and joy, making us feel proud of ourselves. Moreover, it serves as positive reinforcement, encouraging us to keep moving forward. As the famous saying goes, "Success breeds success."

To incorporate this practice into your life, you could start by keeping a 'success journal.' Every day, write down your accomplishments, however small they may seem. Did you make a healthy choice for lunch? Write it down. Did you complete a difficult task at work? Note it. Did you make someone else smile today? Record it. Over time, you'll be surprised at how much you actually achieve on a daily basis.

In addition to celebrating small achievements, it is equally important to celebrate personal milestones. These are significant points in our lives that mark personal growth or accomplishment. For instance, the day you learned to drive, the day you finished a massive project, or the day you finally decluttered your home. These milestones, even if they may seem small or insignificant to others, hold great personal value and significance.

When you celebrate these milestones, you are not just creating joyful memories, but also affirming your personal value, growth and progress. You could celebrate these moments by treating yourself to something special, sharing the joy with loved ones, or simply taking a moment to acknowledge your hard work and persistence.

Questions for self-reflection
1. Can you recall a time when you minimised a personal achievement and what would it look like if you fully celebrated it instead?
2. How might creating a ritual around celebrating small wins affect your overall well-being and motivation?

In conclusion, celebrating small achievements and milestones is a powerful way to foster joy, self-esteem, and motivation. It's a reminder that every step we take towards our goals, no matter how small, is worth recognising and celebrating. This practice allows us to find joy in our journey, not just in reaching the destination.

Embracing simple pleasures is all about finding joy in the ordinary and the everyday. It is about reclaiming play and creativity, indulging in hobbies and passions, and appreciating small victories. As we cultivate these practices, we open ourselves to a world of joy and contentment that lies squarely within our reach.

7
GRATITUDE AND APPRECIATION

Joy is the simplest form of gratitude.

— KARL BARTH

Life can be a beautiful and enriching journey, yet it can also be filled with trials, tribulations, and challenges. Often, it is our perspective towards these experiences that shape our emotions, our mindset, and ultimately our quality of life. This is where the power of gratitude comes in. Gratitude is more than just saying 'thank you.' It is a deeper sense of thankfulness that opens our eyes to the beauty of life in its entirety, with all its ups and downs, joys and sorrows.

Gratitude is a perspective, a way of life, a lens through which we can view our experiences in a positive light. It invites us to focus on abundance rather than lack, on blessings rather than shortcomings, and on growth rather than stagnation. When we live with gratitude, we recognise and appreciate the value in every experience, every encounter, and every moment. We stop taking things for granted and start seeing the beauty in the ordinary.

Living with gratitude can change our lives in beautiful ways. It can improve our emotional well-being, enhance our relationships, boost our resilience, and even contribute to better physical health. It offers a pathway to joy and contentment that does not depend on external circumstances, but on our internal mindset.

In this chapter on Gratitude and Appreciation, we will dive deeper into the concept of gratitude and its significance in building a joyous life. We will explore how to develop a gratitude practice, harness the power of gratitude journaling, and how to cultivate an attitude of appreciation in all areas of life. Through this exploration, we will unlock the power of gratitude and embark on a journey towards a more joyous and fulfilling life.

DEVELOPING A GRATITUDE PRACTICE FOR A POSITIVE MINDSET

Gratitude is a feeling of thankfulness that extends beyond just acknowledging the good in others. Gratitude is about recognising the good in our lives in general, including our experiences, circumstances, and the natural world around us.

Expressing gratitude has been shown[1] to have numerous benefits, from boosting mood and reducing stress to improving sleep and fostering a greater sense of overall happiness. This can be achieved with a daily gratitude practice, such as keeping a gratitude journal or making it a habit to reflect on the things you're thankful for each day.

Gratitude is more than an emotion — it is a habit that we can develop to positively change our mindset and overall life experience. Consistent practice enables us to navigate life's ups and downs with grace, resilience, and positivity, enhancing our ability to experience joy and contentment.

To develop a gratitude practice, start with a simple exercise — pause for a moment each day to consciously reflect on the aspects of your life for which you are grateful. You might choose to do this as you wake up in the morning, setting a positive tone for the day. Alternatively, you could do it at night before you sleep allowing the day's blessings to be your final thoughts before you drift off. This practice helps to shift your focus from worries or stress to appreciation and positivity.

What you reflect on does not have to be monumental. Perhaps you're grateful for the warmth of the sun on your face, a good book, a delicious meal, or a moment of laughter with a friend. Even in challenging times, there is always something to appreciate, even if it is as fundamental as the breath in your lungs, or the sun in the sky.

As you continue this practice, you might start to notice that your perception of daily experiences begins to shift. Situations that you may have previously perceived as mundane or even negative may be seen in a new light as you start to find the silver linings. Traffic during your commute might transform from a source of frustration to an opportunity for solitude and reflection. Challenges at work or in your personal life might change from life's stressors to opportunities for growth and learning.

Remember, the aim of this practice is not to ignore or

dismiss the difficulties in life. It is to balance these difficulties with a conscious recognition of the positive aspects of life, which are often overlooked. The aim is to cultivate a mindset that is better equipped to find joy, even amidst challenges.

Consider incorporating additional practices to further foster gratitude. You might express your appreciation to others more often, regularly volunteer or donate to causes you care about, or practice mindfulness to be fully present in each moment and recognise the blessings it brings.

Developing a gratitude practice takes time and consistency, but its effects are worthwhile. As you train your mind to seek out and focus on the positive, you'll find that joy becomes a more prominent part of your life, regardless of external circumstances. Gratitude, therefore, is a key to unlocking a more joyful and satisfying life.

Questions for self-reflection
1. How might a regular gratitude practice change your outlook on life?
2. What personal barriers have you encountered that might prevent you from fully embracing gratitude, and how might you overcome them?

HARNESSING THE POWER OF GRATITUDE JOURNALING

Gratitude journaling[2] is a powerful tool that can heighten your awareness of the good things in life, fostering a more heartfelt sense of appreciation and joy. This practice involves keeping a dedicated journal to note down the things, people, events, and experiences for which you are thankful. The physical act of writing enhances the cognitive processing of positive emotions, reinforcing the feelings of gratitude.

To harness the power of gratitude journaling, begin by dedicating a specific journal or notebook to this purpose. Try to make this a special and personal item, one that you'll feel drawn to use regularly. It could be a beautifully-bound notebook, a simple pad of paper, or even a digital notepad if you prefer.

Make a habit of writing in your gratitude journal daily. The best time to do this could be in the morning, as a way to start your day positively, or in the evening, reflecting on the blessings of the day. Aim to write down three to five things that you are thankful for each day. These can range from simple pleasures like a cup of your favourite coffee, a phone call with a friend, a good book, or the beauty of a sunset, to more general blessings like good health, family, or personal accomplishments.

As you write in your journal, try to focus on the specifics and the feelings associated with each point. For example, instead of simply writing "I am grateful for my friend," you might say, "I am grateful for the laughter-filled conversation I had with my friend today, which lifted my spirits and made me feel loved and connected." This level of detail helps to deepen your sense of gratitude and reinforce the positive emotions associated with it.

Do not be afraid to include challenges in your gratitude journal. Often, it is through adversity that we grow the most. Instead of focusing on the negative aspects of a difficult situation, try to uncover what you've learned or how you've grown because of it.

Occasionally revisiting past entries can be a source of comfort and a potent reminder of the many blessings in your life, especially on more challenging days. It can show you that good things are continually happening, often outweighing the difficulties.

Gratitude journaling, with regular practice, helps to shift your focus from problems or lack to abundance and positivity, fostering a more joyful and appreciative outlook on life. It can be a valuable practice, to find a quiet space in your day to reconnect with yourself and recognise the many gifts life offers you.

Questions for self-reflection
1. How has the act of writing in a gratitude journal changed your perspective on everyday experiences?
2. Do you find any discernible difference in your mood on days you journal versus days you don't?

EMBRACING AN ATTITUDE OF APPRECIATION IN ALL AREAS OF LIFE

An attitude of appreciation means recognising and valuing the positive aspects present in all areas of life. It is about going beyond the occasional thank-you and developing a deeply embedded mindset of gratitude. Focussing on this perspective of gratitude can significantly enhance your well-being and joy, as it encourages us to focus on life's abundant gifts rather than its challenges.

Appreciation can be applied to every area of life, from relationships and work to self-care and personal growth. Here are some suggestions on how to embrace an attitude of appreciation:

. . .

1. Relationships

Appreciation in relationships involves recognising the value and uniqueness of each person in your life. It means acknowledging the love, support, and joy they bring and expressing your gratitude for it. Regularly tell your loved ones how much they mean to you. Be specific about what you appreciate about them - it could be their kindness, their sense of humour, their patience, or simply their presence in your life.

2. Work

You can cultivate an attitude of appreciation towards your work by focusing on the positive aspects of your job. Recognise the skills and experiences you gain, the purpose it provides, or the people you interact with. Even in a job that isn't ideal, there are lessons to be learned and aspects to be grateful for.

3. Personal Growth

Appreciate the journey of personal growth. Celebrate your accomplishments, no matter how small they may seem. Also, express gratitude for the challenges and failures, for they are your greatest teachers. They provide opportunities to learn, to grow, and to build resilience.

4. Self-care

Show appreciation for yourself and your body by practicing self-care. Recognise the importance of rest, relaxation, and doing activities you love. Be thankful for your body's health, well-being and abilities. Provide it with nourishing food, regular exercise, and adequate rest.

5. Environment

Take the time to appreciate your surroundings. Find beauty in your home, your neighbourhood, and the natural world. Expressing gratitude and appreciation for your environment can lead to an increased desire to care for and preserve it.

> *Questions for self-reflection*
> 1. In which areas of your life has reading about gratitude made the most profound impact?
> 2. How do you plan to sustain your gratitude practice over the long term?

Choosing an attitude of appreciation in all areas of life involves a change in perspective. It means looking for the good in every situation, every person, and every experience. It encourages positivity, resilience, and joy. When gratitude becomes an integral part of your mindset, you'll find that joy is not a fleeting emotion but a stable and sustainable state of being.

In the end, living with gratitude means choosing to focus on the positive aspects of life, no matter how big or small. It is about recognising the good in others, in the world around us, and within ourselves. As we develop this gratitude practice, we create a ripple effect of positivity, enhancing not only our own joy but also spreading it to those around us.

8
LETTING GO OF EXPECTATIONS

Happiness can exist only in acceptance.

— GEORGE ORWELL

Life is a beautiful journey filled with unexpected turns, joyous surprises, and valuable lessons. Yet, sometimes, our own expectations can form invisible chains, limiting our potential to experience and appreciate the multifaceted richness of life. Our preconceived ideas of how things should be can often overshadow the beauty of how things are, hindering our ability to live joyfully and authentically.

In this chapter, we will explore into the intricate ways in which expectations shape our experiences and potentially thwart our happiness. More importantly, we will look into how we can liberate ourselves from these self-imposed constraints to welcome more spontaneity, acceptance, and joy into our lives.

We will examine how accepting imperfections - in ourselves, others, and life situations - can foster resilience and contentment. We will learn to embrace spontaneity, appreciating life's surprises as unique opportunities for growth and enjoyment. Finally, we will discover the power of cultivating a sense of wonder and curiosity, which can help us remain open to life's endless possibilities and find joy in every moment.

The journey of letting go of expectations[1] is an empowering process of self-discovery and transformation. As we release our attachment to how things 'should' be, we create room for appreciating things as they are, ultimately paving the way for a more fulfilled, content, and joyful life. So, let's embark on this exciting journey together.

HOW EXPECTATIONS HINDER JOY

Expectations are the mental preconceptions we have of future events, people, and even ourselves. They act as lenses through which we perceive and interpret our reality. While expectations can sometimes serve as useful guidelines, they can also, paradoxically, prevent us from experiencing the richness and fullness of life. This stems from the fact that expectations inherently involve a projection into the future, which often distracts us from fully engaging with the present moment.

When we cling to our expectations, we create a rigid framework that dictates what our lives should look like. This leaves little room for spontaneous joy and authentic experiences. For example, we may have a fixed idea of how a holiday should be spent. If the reality does not match up with our expectation — perhaps due to bad weather, an unplanned event, or a simple change of plans — it can lead to feelings of disappointment and dissatisfaction. However, if we were open to the experience without pre-set expectations, we might have found joy in unexpected places — the beauty of the rain, the adventure of an unplanned detour, or the simple pleasure of a quiet day indoors.

Expectations not only pertain to events but also to people and ourselves. When we have set ideas about how others should behave, we risk damaging relationships. People are dynamic, and their actions and responses may not always align with our expectations. When this happens, instead of appreciating them for who they are, we might feel let down and upset. Similarly, when we set unrealistic expectations for ourselves — in terms of performance, behaviour, or success — we set ourselves up for disappointment and stress. We might overlook our achievements and growth, focusing instead on the gap between reality and our expectations.

It is crucial to remember that expectations themselves are not inherently harmful. They only become problematic when they are inflexible, unattainable, or don't align with our reality. Therefore, the goal is not to eliminate expectations but rather to hold them lightly. By acknowledging that life is inherently unpredictable and that people, including ourselves, are constantly evolving, we can begin to let go of rigid expectations. This allows us to stay open to the full range of experiences that life has to offer, thereby enhancing our capacity for joy.

Questions for self-reflection
1. In what situations do you find your expectations creating a disconnect between what you hoped for and what is?
2. How do your expectations, when unmet, influence your emotions and perceptions of an experience?

ACCEPTING IMPERFECTIONS

In our journey towards letting go of expectations and cultivating joy, it is essential to embrace the beauty of imperfections[2]. Perfection is an illusion that can create unnecessary pressure and rob us of the present moment's joy. Accepting imperfections means recognising that life is an adventure woven with both triumphs and setbacks, strengths and weaknesses.

By embracing imperfections, we free ourselves from the burden of unrealistic standards and self-judgment. It is a shift towards self-compassion and self-acceptance. Instead of constantly striving for an idealised version of ourselves or others, we learn to appreciate and celebrate our unique qualities, quirks, and flaws. Imperfections are what make us human, relatable, and interesting.

Embracing imperfections also invites authenticity into our lives. When we let go of the need to appear flawless or conform to societal expectations, we create space for genuine connections and relationships. We allow ourselves to be vulnerable, fostering deeper connections with others who appreciate and accept us as we are.

Questions for self-reflection
1. How do you react when confronted with your own imperfections or those of others?
2. In which areas of your life are you hardest on yourself and why?

EMBRACING SPONTANEITY

Spontaneity is the antidote to rigid expectations, offering a sense of freedom and adventure in our lives. It is the willingness to relinquish control and embrace the unknown, opening ourselves to the possibilities that unfold in each moment.

When we embrace spontaneity, we invite new experiences, opportunities, and connections into our lives. It breaks us free from the monotony of routine and the confines of our comfort zones. By stepping into the realm of the unknown, we create space for serendipity and surprise, infusing our lives with freshness, excitement, and joy.

Embracing spontaneity also cultivates resilience and adaptability. Life is unpredictable, and plans often change. When we are flexible and open to spontaneity, we are better equipped to navigate unexpected twists and turns. We learn to dance with life's rhythm, responding to its ever-changing melody with grace and resilience.

Spontaneity also encourages us to be fully present in the moment. It allows us to savour the richness of our experiences, rather than getting caught up in past regrets or future worries. We become more attuned to the beauty and wonder that surround us, finding joy in the simplest of moments.

In letting go of rigid expectations and embracing imperfections and spontaneity, we create space for true joy to flourish. We release the need to control and allow life to unfold with its delightful surprises. By accepting imperfections, we foster self-compassion and invite authenticity into our lives. By embracing spontaneity, we infuse our lives with adventure, resilience, and a deep appreciation for the present moment. Together, these practices pave the way for a more joyous and fulfilling existence.

> *Questions for self-reflection*
> 1. Can you recall a moment when spontaneity led to a cherished memory?
> 2. How might embracing spontaneity in daily life change your overall perspective on unexpected events?

CONNECTING WITH YOUR SENSE OF WONDER AND CURIOSITY

Being able to tap in to our sense of wonder and curiosity is a powerful practice that can reawaken our innate joy and deepen our connection with the world around us. Wonder is the ability to be amazed and fascinated by the mysteries and beauty of life, while curiosity is the thirst for knowledge and the desire to explore and learn. Together, they create a mindset that embraces the awe-inspiring wonders of the universe and invites us to engage with life's limitless possibilities.

1. Embracing wonder

Wonder is a natural human response to the

extraordinary aspects of life. It opens our hearts and minds to the vastness and intricacy of the world, reminding us that there is so much more to discover and appreciate. When we begin to view our world with wonder, we approach life with a sense of humility and reverence, recognising our place within the grandeur of existence.

To embrace wonder, it is important to slow down and observe the world around us. Take a moment to marvel at the intricate patterns in nature, the mesmerising colours of a sunset, or the twinkling stars in the night sky. Allow yourself to be captivated by the beauty and complexity of everyday moments. Cultivate a sense of gratitude for the wonders that surround you, and let that gratitude expand your capacity for joy.

2. Nurturing curiosity

Curiosity is the fuel that drives us to explore, learn, and grow. It is a thirst for knowledge and a desire to understand the world. When we approach life with curiosity, we become active participants in our own experiences. We ask questions, seek answers, and remain open to new perspectives and possibilities.

To nurture curiosity, embrace a mindset of continuous learning. Seek out new experiences, challenge your assumptions, and explore different interests and passions. Engage in activities that pique your curiosity, whether it's reading books, engaging in stimulating conversations, or trying new hobbies. Approach each day with a sense of curiosity, viewing it as an opportunity to learn something new and expand your understanding of the world.

. . .

3. Uniting wonder and curiosity

Wonder and curiosity are closely intertwined, each enhancing the other. When we approach life with wonder, it sparks our curiosity, encouraging us to explore and seek deeper meaning. Conversely, curiosity allows us to uncover the wonders hidden within the ordinary. By embracing both, we create a rich collection of experiences that fuels our joy and deepens our connection with the world.

Together, wonder and curiosity invite us to approach life with childlike eyes, reclaiming the sense of awe and excitement that we may have lost along the way. They remind us that there is always something new to discover, something to be amazed by, and something to appreciate.

Questions for self-reflection
1. What simple wonders have you overlooked recently in your everyday surroundings?
2. How often do you pursue a new curiosity or seek to learn something just for the joy of discovery?

In embracing wonder and curiosity, we infuse our lives with vitality, joy, and a renewed sense of purpose. We awaken to the infinite possibilities that surround us, and in doing so, we tap into the wellspring of joy that lies within our own hearts. Let wonder and curiosity be your guiding companions as you embark on a lifelong journey of exploration, growth, and joy.

Letting go of expectations is not an overnight process — it demands patience, practice, and a great deal of self-compassion. But as we gradually release our grip on how we believe life should be, we open ourselves to experience life as it is - beautiful, unpredictable, and filled with countless opportunities for joy.

9
OVERCOMING OBSTACLES AND BUILDING RESILIENCE

The most beautiful people we have known are those who have known defeat, known suffering, known struggle, known loss, and have found their way out of the depths. These persons have an appreciation, a sensitivity, and an understanding of life that fills them with compassion, gentleness, and a deep loving concern. Beautiful people do not just happen.

— ELISABETH KÜBLER-ROSS

Life is a series of ups and downs, a constant ebb and flow of experiences. Along the path to joy, we inevitably encounter challenges, setbacks, and adversity. However, it is in these difficult times that we have the opportunity to cultivate resilience, learn valuable lessons, and ultimately grow stronger.

The journey through life is as unpredictable as the

weather – bright and sunny one moment and dark and grey the next. For many, the pursuit of joy seems closely tied to chasing constant highs and avoiding the lows. Yet, true joyful living isn't about the absence of adversity but rather finding joy amidst it. In the small, seemingly insignificant moments and the challenges that test our spirit, we can uncover valuable wisdom and grasp at the essence of joyful living.

Modern society, especially in the age of social media, sells us the narrative of perpetual happiness. We see highlight reels, but rarely the behind-the-scenes struggles. This skewed perspective can lead us to believe that joy means a life devoid of challenges. In reality, life's richest lessons and deepest joys are often birthed from overcoming obstacles.

Resilience is our ability to bounce back from setbacks, adapt, and move forward. It is an underrated aspect of joyful living. When we develop resilience, we don't just endure challenges; we transform them into stepping stones towards our own growth. Every setback is an opportunity to refine our perspective, deepen our gratitude, and reaffirm our commitment to finding joy in the little things in our lives, no matter how tumultuous or challenging our life is at any given moment.

Amidst the depths of our struggles, we gain insights that are often elusive during easier times. We learn about our strengths, our values, and the incredible capacity of the human spirit to hope and heal. It is these moments that remind us of the fleeting nature of life, demanding that we savour the simple pleasures and cherish the joys in between.

While it is natural to yearn for ease and continuous upward trajectories, it is really the valleys that shape and define us. Much like a tree that digs its roots deeper during storms to stand tall, we too delve deeper into our core during challenging times, solidifying our foundation and ensuring a more robust growth of our spirit and our own being.

Joyful living is not about filtering out the negatives but embracing life in its entirety. It's about dancing in the rain, finding solace in solitude, and seeing the silver lining in every cloud. The beauty of life lies in its contrasts. When we recognise this, we start to see joy not just in the peaks but also in the valleys, in the everyday, and in the extraordinary.

DEALING WITH CHALLENGES AND SETBACKS ON THE PATH TO JOY

The journey to joy is seldom a straight path. There will be twists and turns, uphill battles, and moments of stumbling. Challenges and setbacks are part and parcel of this journey, but they need not deter you from your destination. This chapter delves into ways to navigate these obstacles and continue on your path to joy.

Questions for self-reflection
1. Can you pinpoint a setback that reshaped your understanding or perspective on joy?
2. How do you keep your internal compass directed towards joy, even during tumultuous periods?

1. Understanding the nature of challenges and setbacks

Challenges come in various forms – personal loss, professional difficulties, health issues, or emotional struggles. No matter what their nature, challenges have a universal trait: they disrupt our comfort zone. Setbacks, on the other hand, occur when we've made progress towards our goals, only to be pushed a few steps back. Both can make us feel overwhelmed and will likely cast a shadow on our journey to joy. However, it is crucial to remember that these obstacles are not potholes but simply stepping stones towards growth.

Questions for self-reflection
1. What forms of adversity have most tested your resilience?
2. How do you usually react when you encounter unexpected setbacks?

2. Acknowledge the obstacle

The first step in dealing with challenges is by acknowledging them. It is natural to feel a range of emotions - from anger to fear, from sadness to confusion. Give yourself permission to feel these emotions without judgment. Denying the reality can lead to greater stress and prevent us from dealing with the situation effectively.

In our attempt to maintain a positive outlook, we sometimes downplay or ignore the difficulties we are facing. While it is crucial to stay positive, it is equally essential to acknowledge that you are going through a tough time. Denying the reality of your situation can lead to greater stress and anxiety. So, give yourself permission to accept the obstacles. Feel your emotions fully—whether they are confusion, anger, sorrow, or fear. Let them flow through you without judgment. This acceptance does not mean you're succumbing to the situation; it means you're accepting that it is what it is and in doing so, you're also preparing to deal with it effectively.

Questions for self-reflection
1. Are there any current challenges in your life that you might be downplaying or ignoring?
2. How do you ensure that you're authentically processing and addressing your emotions during tough times?

3. Change your perspective

Perception plays a significant role in how we approach challenges. If you see these obstacles as insurmountable, they will seem daunting. But if you can view them as opportunities for self-improvement, they will become less intimidating. This is not about denying the hardship, but about finding the silver lining that can guide you towards personal growth and solutions.

The lens through which you view your challenges can make a substantial difference. If you see them as insurmountable hurdles, they will likely appear overwhelming. But if you regard them as opportunities for growth and self-improvement, your mindset starts to shift. Ask yourself: "What can I learn from this situation? How can this strengthen me?" This reframing is not about denying the difficulty of the situation but about finding a silver lining that can guide you towards solutions and personal growth.

Questions for self-reflection
1. When faced with obstacles, how do you actively search for the silver lining?
2. Can you think of a recent challenge that, when viewed from a different angle, presented an opportunity?

4. Take action

Once you have recognised the challenge and changed your perspective, it is time to act. Formulate a practical plan to tackle the problem at hand. The key is to keep moving forward, even if all you can manage is just a small step every single day. Remember, it is the sum of these small steps that will lead to significant changes.

This does not mean that you have to resolve the entire situation immediately. Taking action might be seeking support from friends, family, or a professional. It might be taking time to care for yourself to recharge and build your resilience. It might be devising a practical step-by-step plan to address the issue at hand. The key is to not remain passive but to take intentional steps, however small they might be, towards overcoming your obstacle.

> Questions for self-reflection
> 1. How do you decide on the best course of action when facing a challenge?
> 2. What proactive steps have you recently taken to overcome an obstacle?

5. Stay flexible

The path to joy is a winding, meandering one not a straight, linear path. Be open to changes and willing to adjust your plan as required. If one approach doesn't work, try another. Patience and adaptability are key to overcoming challenges and setbacks.

Stay open and flexible to changes. Your plan might not work the way you initially thought, and that's okay. Adaptability is an essential part of resilience and a powerful tool in overcoming obstacles. Be ready to revise your plan, explore different avenues, and stay patient and gentle with yourself. Each step, no matter how small, is progress on your journey to joy.

Questions for self-reflection
1. How have you had to adjust your plans recently in response to unforeseen challenges?
2. What practices or strategies do you employ to maintain adaptability in the face of adversity?

6. Celebrate every small victory

No matter how small, celebrate each victory. Acknowledging your achievements, no matter how minor they may seem, fuels your journey and keeps you inspired and motivated. Each victory, each hurdle crossed, brings you a step closer to joy.

This journey through life can be undoubtedly tough, and it is crucial to acknowledge every bit of progress you make. Celebrate your small victories, as they are signs of your strength and resilience. Did you make it through a difficult day? Did you manage to accomplish a small task that seemed impossible a little while ago? Celebrate that! These moments of triumph fuel your journey and keep you turned in the direction of where you are heading.

Questions for self-reflection
1. What recent small achievement of yours went unrecognised or uncelebrated?
2. How do celebrations, even for minor successes, influence your motivation and drive?

A much loved, very brave friend, Kate was recently diagnosed with FND. The acronym stands for Functional Neurological Disorder. It is somewhat a blanket term that doctors fall back on when there is a neurological dysfunction somewhere in the brain that they cannot quite pinpoint yet. Although the wiring is intact, there seems to be an issue with how the synapses are transmitted.

In Kate's case, FND left her with speech and some movement defects. She began to stutter and slurred her words and sometimes blanked out whenever she felt stressed. It took her a while to come to grips with the diagnosis, which unfortunately was a lot both to take in and to adjust to.

In the end though, she decided to embrace her diagnosis even if she could not change it. She started sharing her journey and sharing her thoughts, frustrations, her good days and bad days. She not only found a dedicated following and people who comforted and commiserated but also many who admired her boldness and her bravery.

Remember, the journey to joy is a personal one, and each person's path will look different. It is about finding what works for you and understanding that challenges and setbacks are not hindrances but integral parts of your journey. They are opportunities to learn, grow, and become the best version of yourself.

BUILDING RESILIENCE — YOUR INNER POWER

"Fall seven times, stand up eight.' Proverb

Resilience is the ability to bounce back from difficulties. It is a skill that can be learned and nurtured. By taking care of your physical, emotional, and mental well-being, by maintaining a positive outlook, and by seeking support when necessary, you can build your resilience. This inner strength will be your ally in overcoming challenges and setbacks on your path to joy.

Life will always present us with challenges and setbacks. But these obstacles don't have to halt our journey. In acknowledging the challenges, changing our perspectives, taking action, remaining flexible, and celebrating our progress, we can navigate these obstacles and continue on our path to joy. Remember, the journey itself is a part of joy, and every challenge we overcome is a testament to our strength and resilience.

Questions for self-reflection
1. When have you felt your resilience was at its strongest, and what contributed to that feeling?
2. What challenges have you faced that made you recognise the importance of nurturing your inner power?

1. Building a support network

We are social creatures by nature, and having a network of support is pivotal in maintaining emotional health and resilience. This network, usually made up of family, friends, mentors, even professional counsellors, offers the support, encouragement, guidance, and the listening ear we often need during challenging times.

Opening up about our experiences and seeking the wisdom of these connections can be therapeutic in itself. Not only does it instil a sense of solace, knowing that someone genuinely cares, but it also opens doors to invaluable insights and coping strategies.

By actively leaning on and learning from our support network, we enrich our emotional toolbox, ensuring that we become better prepared to face life's inevitable ups and downs. Sharing your experiences and seeking their perspectives can provide a sense of comfort and help you gather valuable insights and learn coping mechanisms.

Questions for self-reflection
1. Who are the two most crucial individuals in your support network and why do they hold that significance?
2. How do you actively ensure you're both giving and receiving within your support network?

2. Practicing self-compassion and self-care

When things go wrong, and we find ourselves in challenging situations, that is often when we are hardest on ourselves. Treating ourselves with kindness and compassion during difficult times is essential practice for resilience.

It is important to acknowledge and accept that setbacks and challenges are simply a part of life and that it is completely normal to experience a whole range of emotions. Find the space to give yourself the compassion, understanding and forgiveness you'd offer a dear friend. By embracing your own invaluable humanness, you also allow yourself the room to heal and grow.

Beyond merely acknowledging the need for kindness towards yourself, it is imperative to actively incorporate self-care into your daily routines. Such practices, when regularly integrated, serve as anchors, grounding us and ensuring the holistic health of our body, mind, and spirit. Carving out dedicated moments in our schedules for activities that invigorate us, whether that's diving into cherished hobbies, immersing ourselves in the healing embrace of nature, or indulging in deep introspection, can act as restorative oases amidst the desert of life's challenges.

Understanding that self-care is not just an occasional indulgence but a necessary investment is essential. While it is delightful to occasionally lose oneself in hobbies or participate in nature retreats, it is equally important to recognise when professional guidance might be beneficial. Seeking professional assistance, whether it is therapy-based or counselling, is not a sign of weakness but rather an acknowledgment of our humanity and an affirmation of our commitment to our own well-being. By consistently prioritising self-care and understanding its multi-faceted nature, we learn to build our resilience and foster an environment within us that is conducive to joy, growth, and long lasting well-being.

Questions for self-reflection
1. How do you respond to your own mistakes, and what is one step that you can take to treat yourself with more compassion?
2. What is one self-care activity that makes you feel most rejuvenated, and how often do you prioritise it?

3. Developing coping mechanisms

Knowing yourself well and finding out what works best for you in times of stress and difficulty helps you to build an arsenal of coping strategies. There may be a range of different ways to react and respond to challenging times but it is vital to learn and develop healthy coping mechanisms that resonate most with you personally.

Learning how to manage your emotions and thoughts, prioritising your own well-being and mental health will all help you to build resilience over time. Activities that help reduce stress, such as exercise, mindfulness, journaling, or practicing relaxation techniques are also essential to keep your mental and physical health in good shape.. These strategies also help manage your emotions, promote well-being, and build resilience over time.

Questions for self-reflection
1. Which coping mechanism has had the most positive impact on your well-being recently?
2. Are there situations where you've found certain coping mechanisms to be ineffective, and how did you adjust?

4. Maintaining a positive mindset

While positivity has been given a bad name lately, the ability to tune in to a positive outlook is valuable. Having a positive mindset does not mean ignoring the negative nor pretending that challenges don't exist, instead it really is about focusing more on solutions rather than dwelling on problems.

Working to reframe challenges as opportunities for growth and learning allows you to take a different more self-serving perspective. We can tap into optimism by practicing appreciation and gratitude and shifting your attention to the things that are going well in your life. A positive mindset can fuel your resilience, enabling you to bounce back from difficult times.

Questions for self-reflection
1. Can you recall a recent situation where maintaining a positive mindset changed the outcome for you?
2. How do you handle situations where it is challenging to see the positive side?

5. Seeking meaning and purpose

Our individual journeys through life are often guided by the invisible compass of our core values, passions, and the deeper purpose that we believe drives our existence. Diving into introspection and genuinely recognising what drives us, what we stand for, and what brings meaning to our lives can illuminate our path, especially during the murkier, more challenging phases of life.

When we have clarity on what truly matters, it becomes easier to navigate challenges. We learn to view life's challenges not as obstacles but as essential chapters that add depth, colour and understanding to our story. This perspective doesn't just offer direction — it infuses our journey with a sense of purpose and passion.

However, it's not just about recognising these driving forces, it is also about maintaining a strong connection to them. In the face of adversity, this ability to connect to our inner compass becomes an invaluable asset. When we tether ourselves to our sense of purpose, our resilience is not just about bouncing back, it's about moving forward with conviction and determination. This deep-seated connection not only helps us overcome hardships but transforms them into powerful lessons, enriching our journey and reinforcing our commitment to the values and passions that define us.

Questions for self-reflection
1. How would you define your current purpose in life, and has it evolved over the years?
2. Can you think of an instance where your sense of purpose helped guide you through a tough decision or challenge?

6. Practicing adaptability

In a world that is in a state of constant change, the capacity to be adaptable becomes a highly valuable trait. Resilience does not mean stubbornly sticking to one path even when it is leading you astray, it means having the flexibility to recognise when change is necessary. When life throws curveballs, those who are adaptable do not get bogged down by rigidity or held back by preconceived notions. Instead, they approach situations with an open mind, ready to consider alternative perspectives and solutions.

Being open-minded means that you are not just waiting for the next obstacle but are proactively seeking growth and opportunities in every situation. It is not merely about survival, but about thriving and making the most out of every experience. With adaptability in your toolkit, not only do you become more resilient in the face of adversity, but you also open doors to possibilities you may not have previously considered. Life's unexpected moments, instead of being daunting, can become unique opportunities for personal growth.

With these practices, resilience can be nurtured and

strengthened over time. It's a powerful internal resource that allows us to navigate life's challenges, learn from them, and emerge stronger and wiser. So, remember, every time you fall, you have the capacity to rise again, stronger than before.

Questions for self-reflection
1. What was a recent situation where you had to be particularly adaptable, and what did you learn from it?
2. How do you handle moments of unexpected change or when things don't go according to plan?

In overcoming obstacles and building resilience, we embark on a journey of change. Challenges become opportunities for growth, setbacks become stepping stones, and adversity becomes a catalyst for personal development. By harnessing our inner strength, embracing the lessons, and maintaining a resilient mindset, we learn to navigate the twists and turns of life with grace and perseverance, ultimately finding joy even in the face of adversity.

10

CREATING YOUR JOYFUL LIFE

Let your joy be in your journey—not in some distant goal.

— TIM COOK

Creating a joyful life requires intentionality, mindfulness, and a genuine commitment to personal well-being. By consciously choosing to incorporate joy and gratitude into our everyday lives, designing a personal joy plan, and nurturing joy in ourselves and in others, we begin to create a lifestyle that radiates positivity, fulfilment, and contentment.

INTEGRATING JOY AND GRATITUDE INTO DAILY LIFE

In Chapter 7, we looked at what gratitude and appreciation is and how to develop a gratitude practice. Here we will look at how we can incorporate it as an on-going practise in to our daily lives. When we pay attention, we naturally find that our lives are filled with opportunities for joy and gratitude. To make the most of these opportunities, we must first recognise them and then intentionally incorporate them into our everyday routine.

Start by making time each day to acknowledge the things that do bring you joy. It might be as simple as a cup of your favourite coffee in the morning, a walk in the park, or a heartwarming conversation with a friend. Paying attention to these moments and consciously savouring them enhances our experience of joy.

1. Being grateful to others

Being thankful for others is not always something that usually comes easily or naturally to us. But expressing your appreciation and gratitude to others can help to reinforce your own feelings of thankfulness but can also spread joy. Take the time to thank the people in your life for their kindness, support, or companionship. This can strengthen your relationships and create a positive feedback loop of gratitude and joy.

2. Savouring joyful moments

When you've identified the moments that bring you joy, take your time to savour them. For instance, if you enjoy your morning coffee, don't just gulp it down. Sit down, taste it, smell it, and fully immerse yourself in the experience. This practice of savouring will enhance your joy and make each experience much more memorable.

· · ·

3. Creating joyful rituals

Integrating joy and gratitude can also involve creating daily rituals that celebrate them. These rituals can be as simple or complex as you like. For example, you might start your day by writing in your gratitude journal and end it by spending a few minutes reflecting on the joyful moments of your day. These rituals can help anchor your day in positivity and joy.

4. Maintaining a Joyful Environment

Your environment plays an important role in your mood and your emotions. Create an environment that supports your happiness by surrounding yourself with things that bring you joy, like photos of loved ones, favourite books, or plants. Regularly decluttering and organising your space can also enhance feelings of satisfaction and control and contribute to your overall joy.

By incorporating these practices into your daily life, you will slowly gain a more joyful and grateful outlook. Remember, the goal is not to ignore life's difficulties but to make a conscious effort to focus on the positive and find joy in the everyday. Over time, these practices can transform your perspective, helping you lead a more joyful and satisfying life.

Questions for self-reflection
1. How do you feel when someone expresses their genuine gratitude towards you?
2. Are there any moments when you felt the need to thank someone but hesitated? Why?

DESIGNING A PERSONAL JOY PLAN FOR LONG-TERM HAPPINESS

Creating a lifestyle of joy requires more than just moment-to-moment mindfulness; it also necessitates a long-term plan. A personal joy plan is a roadmap that guides you toward more happiness and fulfilment in life.

To create this plan, begin by identifying your values, passions, and goals. What brings you joy? What gives you a sense of purpose? How do you want to grow as a person? Once you've identified these elements, incorporate them into your plan.

Set actionable and achievable goals that align with your vision of a joyful life. These goals could be related to personal growth, relationships, career, health, hobbies, or any other area of life that is important to you.Remember, the goal of your plan isn't to create a perfect life but to increase your overall joy and satisfaction. It should be flexible and adaptable, changing as you grow and as your circumstances change.

A Personal Joy Plan is a proactive approach to cultivating happiness and contentment in your life. It involves identifying what brings you joy, setting achievable goals, and taking tangible steps to incorporate more joy into your life.

The following steps help you create your own Personal Joy Plan:

1. Identify your joy triggers

Start by identifying what brings you joy. This could be activities you enjoy, people you love spending time with, places you feel happiest, or personal achievements that fill you with pride. Everyone's joy triggers are unique, so take some time to explore and understand your own.

Once you have started to identify the things that please and uplift you, Write them down in a list or in your journal. If you are a scrapbook enthusiast, consider dedicating some pages to these greatest joys, complete with decorations and photographs - making sure that every time you see flick through your scrapbook you would be uplifted.

2. Set joy goals

With your joy triggers in mind, set some goals that align with these triggers. If spending time in nature brings you joy, for example, a goal could be to spend at least an hour a week outdoors. If connecting with others brings you happiness, your goal could be to reach out to a friend or family member every day. These goals should be specific, measurable, achievable, relevant, and time-bound (SMART) to increase their effectiveness.

3. Create a joyful routine

Incorporate activities that bring you joy into your daily or weekly routine. This could mean setting aside time each morning for a hobby you love, scheduling regular catch-ups with friends, or setting up your workspace in a way that brings you joy. By making these activities a regular part of your routine, you ensure that joy is a consistent aspect of your life.

4. Prioritise self-care

Self-care plays a crucial role in maintaining long-term happiness. It is essential to look after your physical, emotional, and mental well-being. Regular exercise, a healthy diet, adequate sleep, and relaxation techniques such as mindfulness or meditation can all contribute to your overall sense of joy and well-being.

5. Reflect and adjust accordingly

Regularly reflect on your Personal Joy Plan. Consider. Consider what's working well and what might need to be adjusted. Perhaps a goal you set is no longer relevant, or maybe you've discovered a new joy trigger. Adjust your plan as needed to ensure it continues to serve you.

6. Stay flexible and patient

Understand that a Personal Joy Plan is not about achieving a constant state of happiness. Life naturally has ups and downs, and it is normal to experience negative emotions. The goal is to have a system that encourages you to intentionally seek and savour joy whenever it is possible.

Creating a Personal Joy Plan is a dynamic process that evolves with you. It is a commitment to consciously prioritising joy and well-being in your life. By identifying your joy triggers, setting achievable goals, and regularly reflecting on your progress, you can cultivate a lifestyle that fosters long-term happiness.

Questions for self-reflection
1. How do you track and celebrate the small victories towards your long-term joy goals?
2. Are there specific areas or domains in your life where you struggle to find joy? How can you approach them differently?

SHARING JOY WITH OTHERS

Joy is a renewable resource — the more we experience, the more we have to share with others. By nurturing joy in ourselves, we can positively influence the people around us, creating a ripple effect that can spread far beyond our immediate environment.

While your Personal Joy Plan is the perfect roadmap to ensuring that you live in more purposeful joy, being able to share and encourage joy in others is a gift that is often returned many times over. When you have found joy, and you feel secure and confident in your own ability to seek out moments of joy in your life, you can begin to share this positive outlook and experience with others. There are a number of ways in which you can do this:

1. Practice kindness

Small acts of kindness are the simplest and most direct ways of sharing joy. Whether it's lending a helping hand, sharing a warm smile, or simply being there to listen, your kindness can help brighten someone else's day. The practise of kindness, is one in which you take the time to consider another's needs and desires. It requires us to consider another's circumstances and situations and how we might help to ease their challenges.

Of course, it does not fall on us to make things better for another, that can only be achieved themselves. However we can be available, to provide support and strength when it is required.

2. Share your positivity

Despite the bad rep positivity gets (toxic positivity), being able to focus on the positive makes a significant difference to our outlooks and our lives. It is not about learning to ignore the negative but to maintain constant and consistent focus on the positive. In life, negative experiences are inevitable. Even so, how to choose to think about and respond to those experiences are what makes the most difference in our lives.

When a challenge arises in a friend's life, it might be in the form of a tight deadline, a difficult co-worker, or even a family loss, it is not beneficial for them if they wallow and feel sorry for themselves continuously. However, while it is important to acknowledge the sadness and the trauma, at the appropriate time, it is also important to then also face forward and focus on different ways to feel better.

When we share our positive outlook and experiences with others, it helps foster a positive environment for them and also within ourselves. This then often leads to a closeness and a connection through a shared experience of joy.

3. Support others

Being able to be there for others during their times of

need is a gift. While offering support and showing empathy can bring comfort and joy to those facing tough times, it also brings immense value and satisfaction to you too. In recognising another and helping them in their time of need, we often find value and purpose in our sense of self and even in the sometimes challenging experiences we may have faced in our own lives.

When we have lived through a difficult experience, we are often able to talk about it and share our experience of it with someone who may be experiencing the same. The kind of support that you can offer that comes from your own person experience is invaluable. While we may have learnt and grown through our challenges, being able to share our lessons and 'things we now know' directly, often brings a personal gratification and satisfaction to our personal sense of purpose.

4. Celebrate others

It is natural to ask 'why not me?' when we are confronted with someone else's success. It might feel as if we deserve that success too. There may be a thousand and one reasons someone has found success and you haven't, the key is not to dwell on 'why not me?' and learn to celebrate the achievements and successes of others.

Being open and willing to share genuine happiness for someone else's success and joy makes you a generous, kind, loving person. When you are able to look at another's success as a part of everyone's achievements, you become open to embracing joy in the myriad of ways it might present itself, even if it is not for you personally.

Remember, joy is not a zero-sum game. The more you

share, the more joy comes back to you. By nurturing joy within yourself and spreading it to others, you contribute to a more positive, joyful world while enhancing your own value, purpose and inherent self-worth.

> *Questions for self-reflection*
> 1. Can you think of a recent moment when sharing your joy with someone else magnified the experience for you?
> 2. How do you handle situations when others might not perceive or resonate with your source of joy?

BUILDING YOUR JOYFUL LIFESTYLE

As we reach the end of this chapter on creating a joyful lifestyle, it's crucial to remember that joy is an ongoing journey, not a destination. The strategies shared throughout this chapter, from integrating joy and gratitude into daily life, designing a personal joy plan, to nurturing joy in yourself and spreading it to others, are all stepping stones on the path to a more joyful existence.

Choosing to live a joyful lifestyle is a deeply personal and unique experience. What brings joy to one person may not have the same effect on another. As such, it's essential to personalise your journey to joy, aligning your actions and choices with your values, passions, and with what genuinely brings you joy.

Remember a joyful lifestyle is not about ignoring life's challenges or difficulties. It is about developing the ability to find joy amid adversity, celebrating life's simple pleasures, and fostering a mindset of gratitude. It's about embracing the potential for growth inherent in our struggles and using these opportunities to nurture our resilience and strengthen our joy.

In the grand scheme of things though, it is not the pursuit of constant happiness that matters most, but the intentional effort to seek and spread joy wherever and whenever we can. Through our outlook, actions and attitudes, we have the power to create a ripple effect of joy that extends from our personal lives into the lives of others.

As you move forward, remember to be patient with yourself. Change never happens overnight, but each step you take towards joy is a step in the right direction. Keep exploring, experimenting, and adapting your approach as you learn what works best for you.

Questions for self-reflection
1. What challenges have you encountered in your pursuit of a joyful lifestyle, and how did you overcome them?
2. How do you keep yourself motivated and committed to building a life filled with joy, especially during times when joy feels distant?

The path to joy is yours to create. Embrace the journey, savour the moments of happiness along the way, and remember: even the smallest changes can lead to a more joyful lifestyle. Here's to your journey toward a life filled with more joy, fulfilment, and happiness.

11
REFLECTION AND CELEBRATION

The more you praise and celebrate your life, the more there is in life to celebrate.

— OPRAH WINFREY

As we approach the end of this journey, it is time to pause, reflect, and celebrate. This journey of finding joy in the little things, overcoming obstacles, building resilience, and fostering a joyful lifestyle is a deeply personal one. It has very likely uncovered layers of understanding, given rise to new perspectives, and triggered significant growth within. The aim of this chapter is to guide you through reflecting on your journey, sharing your experiences, and most importantly, celebrating your accomplishments.

REFLECTING ON THE JOURNEY

The process of finding joy in the little things is life-changing. It shifts your focus from the big, often unattainable ideals of happiness, to appreciating the everyday moments of joy that are easily and continuously within our reach. Take time to reflect on how this change in perspective has impacted your life.

Perhaps you've noticed an increased awareness of the world around you, a heightened sense of gratitude, or a deeper appreciation for life's simple pleasures. Maybe you've discovered joy triggers that you never realised existed, or you've been surprised at how much joy can be found in the seemingly mundane.

As you reflect, take a moment to acknowledge how your understanding of joy has evolved and how this newfound awareness has enriched your daily life. This is not an endpoint, but a new beginning, a solid foundation upon which to continue building your joyful life.

Reflection is a powerful tool that helps us understand the progress we have made, appreciate the growth we have experienced, and recognise the changes we have undergone. As you reflect on your journey of finding joy in the little things, you're invited to delve deep into your experiences and insights.

To begin with, think about the way you perceived joy before you started this journey. You might refer back to your self-reflection questions and see how you defined your experience of joy — What did joy mean to you then? Was it tied to significant life events or achievements? Now, contrast this with your current understanding of joy. How has it evolved? Perhaps you've discovered that joy is not just found in the grand, remarkable events of life but also in its ordinary, seemingly mundane moments.

Consider the small things that have given you joy recently. It could be a quiet morning cup of coffee, a heartfelt conversation with a friend, or even the simple act of curling up with a good book. Reflect on the sense of contentment these experiences brought you, their simplicity notwithstanding.

This journey will hopefully have increased your awareness and appreciation of the world around you. As you continued to look for joy in the little things, you may have started noticing the beauty in everyday moments, the kindness in familiar faces, and the pleasure in routine activities. This shift in awareness is a significant part of your personal change in perspective, leading to a more mindful and joyful way of living.

Reflect, too, on the resilience you have developed in this process. As you have learned to find joy in the little things, you've likely become better equipped to handle life's challenges. You have realised that even in tough times, small pockets of joy can still be found, providing comfort and reinforcing your inner strength.

Looking back, you might notice a change in your overall happiness and contentment. By recognising and celebrating the small, joyful moments in your everyday life, you have begun to focus on a more sustained and resilient form of happiness. One that is not dependent on external circumstances but is rooted in your capacity to recognise and appreciate life's simple pleasures.

In this reflection, acknowledge and honour your growth. It is a testament to your openness to change, your willingness to shift your perspective, and your commitment to fostering a more joyful and fulfilling life. Remember, the insights you gain through this reflection are not the end of your journey but are stepping stones leading you further along your path of personal growth and joy.

> *Questions for self-reflection*
> 1. How did your initial perceptions of joy differ from the joy you've discovered in everyday moments?
> 2. Can you recall a seemingly mundane moment that unexpectedly brought you great joy?

SHARING PERSONAL INSIGHTS AND EXPERIENCES

Sharing your experiences is a powerful tool for reflection and growth. It allows you to express your thoughts, insights, and feelings, further solidifying your understanding and enhancing your learning process.

Take some time to share your journey with others. It could be through conversation with a trusted friend or family member, journaling your thoughts and experiences, or even sharing your insights on a social media platform. Whichever method you choose, sharing your journey not only helps you reflect on your personal growth but could inspire others to embark on their journey to joy.

Sharing your personal insights and experiences is not only a cathartic exercise that promotes self-reflection but also serves as a means of connecting with others, potentially inspiring them to embark on their own journeys to joy. It helps to bring your personal, often introspective journey into the social world, further enriching your understanding and perspective.

1. Dialogue

Begin by sharing your experiences with trusted friends or family members. This can be an informal conversation over coffee, a dedicated heart-to-heart session, or even an ongoing dialogue over time. Encourage them to share their experiences and insights in return, fostering a mutual exchange that can yield fresh perspectives and deeper understanding.

2. Journalling

Journalling is an effective way to express your thoughts, feelings, and experiences. It offers a private space for unfiltered self-expression, allowing you to explore your journey in depth. You can record the moments of joy you have discovered, the challenges you have encountered, the lessons you have learned, and the growth you have experienced. Journalling is not only a record of your journey but also a tool for self-reflection and growth.

3. Digital Sharing

In our increasingly digital world, you can also choose to share your journey on social media platforms or on personal blogs. This can help you connect with a broader audience, creating a space for shared experiences and mutual inspiration. Remember, the goal is not to project an image of perfection, but to honestly share your journey with its ups and downs, thereby encouraging others to embrace their own journey to joy.

. . .

4. Community Groups

Consider joining or even forming a local or online group focussed on personal growth and joy. Sharing in a group setting can foster a sense of community, offer diverse perspectives, and provide mutual support and encouragement. Such a group can provide a safe haven for people on similar journeys, where everyone can share, learn, and grow together.

Sharing your personal insights and experiences deepens your own understanding and helps others on their journey. Whether you choose to share in an intimate conversation with a friend, write in your personal journal, post on a blog or social media, or participate in a community group, remember that sharing is an essential part of your journey to joy, as it provides an opportunity for reflection, growth, and connection.

> *Questions for self-reflection*
> 1. Which method of sharing your experiences resonates most deeply with you and why?
> 2. What emotions or insights surfaced when you shared your journey with others, whether privately or publicly?

CELEBRATING GROWTH, GRATITUDE, AND THE NEWFOUND JOY WITHIN

Every step you have taken on this journey is worth celebrating. Even if the path was rocky at times, even if you stumbled or strayed, the very act of embarking on this journey is a testament to your courage, your openness, and your commitment to your own personal growth.

Celebrate your increased resilience, your ability to find lessons in adversity, and the myriad ways you have now incorporated joy and gratitude into your daily life. Whether it is through a quiet moment of reflection, a self-care day, or even a joyful dance in your living room, take some time to truly celebrate your achievements.

More importantly, take a moment to acknowledge the newfound joy within you. This joy, borne out of intentional living, self-exploration, and a commitment to personal growth, is a powerful force. It is a light that can brighten the darkest days, a strength that can weather the toughest storms, and a guide that can lead you towards a fulfilling, happy life.

Questions for self-reflection
1. Which specific moments during your journey have evoked the strongest feelings of gratitude in you?
2. As you recognise and celebrate the joy within you, what's one word that encapsulates your current state of being?

Remember that the journey towards joy is an ongoing process, one that continues to unfold with each passing day. For now, take a deep breath, reflect on how far you've come, and celebrate the joyous, resilient individual you've become. Congratulations your journey, your growth, and the radiant joy that now resides within you!

REFERENCES

1. INTRODUCTION TO JOYFUL LIVING

1. McKee LG, Algoe SB, Faro AL, O'Leary JL, O'Neal CW. *Picture This! Bringing joy into Focus and Developing Healthy Habits of Mind*: Rationale, design, and implementation of a randomized control trial for young adults. Contemp Clin Trials Commun. 2019 Jun 29;15:100391. doi: 10.1016/j.conctc.2019.100391. PMID: 31372571; PMCID: PMC6658827.
2. Tugade MM, Fredrickson BL. Resilient individuals use positive emotions to bounce back from negative emotional experiences. J Pers Soc Psychol. 2004 Feb;86(2):320-33. doi: 10.1037/0022-3514.86.2.320. PMID: 14769087; PMCID: PMC3132556.
3. Kimmerer, R W.Braiding Sweetgrass. Milkweed Editions, 2015.

2. MINDFUL AWARENESS

1. Brazier, D (2013) Mindfulness reconsidered, European Journal of Psychotherapy & Counselling, 15:2, 116-126, DOI: 10.1080/13642537.2013.795335
2. Perciavalle V, Blandini M, Fecarotta P, Buscemi A, Di Corrado D, Bertolo L, Fichera F, Coco M. The role of deep breathing on stress. Neurol Sci. 2017 Mar;38(3):451-458. doi: 10.1007/s10072-016-2790-8. Epub 2016 Dec 19. PMID: 27995346.
3. Nhất Hạnh, T.. The miracle of mindfulness : a manual on meditation. Boston :Beacon Press,1987
4. Keng SL, Smoski MJ, Robins CJ. Effects of mindfulness on psychological health: a review of empirical studies. Clin Psychol Rev. 2011 Aug;31(6):1041-56. doi: 10.1016/j.cpr.2011.04.006. Epub 2011 May 13. PMID: 21802619; PMCID: PMC3579190.

3. NATURE'S BEAUTY

1. Wilson EO.*Biophilia*. Cambridge: Harvard University Press, 1984.
2. Seymour, V. The Human-Nature Relationship and its impact on health: A critical review. Front. Public Health 2016 Volume 4 - 2016 |https://doi.org/10.3389/fpubh.2016.00260
3. Howell AJ, Dopko RL, Passmore HA, Buro K. Nature connectedness: associations with well-being and mindfulness.*Pers Individ Dif*(2011) 51:166–71.

    Barton J, Pretty J. What is the best dose of nature and green exercise for improving mental health - A multi study analysis.*Environ Sci Technol*(2010) 44:3947–55. doi:10.1021/es903183r
4. Brown DK, Barton JL, Gladwell VF. Viewing nature scenes positively affects recovery of autonomic function following acute-mental stress. Environ Sci Technol. 2013 Jun 4;47(11):5562-9. doi: 10.1021/es305019p. Epub 2013 May 16. PMID: 23590163; PMCID: PMC3699874.
5. Furuyashiki A, Tabuchi K, Norikoshi K, Kobayashi T, Oriyama S. A comparative study of the physiological and psychological effects of forest bathing (Shinrin-yoku) on working age people with and without depressive tendencies. Environ Health Prev Med. 2019 Jun 22;24(1):46. doi: 10.1186/s12199-019-0800-1. PMID: 31228960; PMCID: PMC6589172.

    Hansen MM, Jones R, Tocchini K. Shinrin-Yoku (Forest Bathing) and Nature Therapy: A State-of-the-Art Review. Int J Environ Res Public Health. 2017 Jul 28;14(8):851. doi: 10.3390/ijerph14080851. PMID: 28788101; PMCID: PMC5580555.
6. Kim, S., Son, S. Y., Kim, M. J., Lee, C. H., & Park, S. (2022). Physiological Responses of Adults during Soil-mixing Activities Based on the Presence of Soil Microorganisms: A Metabolomics Approach.*Journal of the American Society for Horticultural Science*,147(3), 135-144. Retrieved Aug 9, 2023, from https://doi.org/10.21273/JASHS05146-21
7. Zhao H, Zhang H, Xu Y, He W, Lu J. Why Are People High in Dispositional Awe Happier? The Roles of Meaning in Life and Materialism. Front Psychol. 2019 May 22;10:1208. doi: 10.3389/fpsyg.2019.01208. PMID: 31191402; PMCID: PMC6540826.

4. EVERYDAY MOMENTS: MAKING THE ORDINARY EXTRAORDINARY

1. Mindful Eating https://www.hsph.harvard.edu/nutritionsource/mindful-eating/. Accessed 2 Sept 2023.
2. Robinson E, Aveyard P, Daley A, Jolly K, Lewis A, Lycett D, Higgs S. Eating attentively: a systematic review and meta-analysis of the effect of food intake memory and awareness on eating. Am J Clin Nutr. 2013 Apr;97(4):728-42. doi: 10.3945/ajcn.112.045245. Epub 2013 Feb 27. PMID: 23446890; PMCID: PMC3607652.

5. MEANINGFUL CONNECTIONS: THE JOY IN TOGETHERNESS

1. Social relationships and health https://www.science.org/doi/abs/10.1126/science.3399889
   Accessed 2 Sept 2023.
2. Good genes are nice, but joy is better. https://news.harvard.edu/gazette/story/2017/04/over-nearly-80-years-harvard-study-has-been-showing-how-to-live-a-healthy-and-happy-life/ A accessed 12 Sept 2023
3. The Science of Kindness https://www.cedars-sinai.org/blog/science-of-kindness.html. Accessed 2 Sept 2023

6. SIMPLE PLEASURES

1. Journal of Play in Adulthood
   https://www.journalofplayinadulthood.org.uk
2. Neale, D, The golden age of play in adults,
   https://www.bps.org.uk/psychologist/golden-age-play-adults
   Accessed 2 Sept 2023
3. Quinn, J, How Learning a new hobby can help you find your state of flow https://chopra.com/articles/how-learning-a-new-hobby-can-help-you-find-your-flow-state Accessed 2 Sept 2023

7. GRATITUDE AND APPRECIATION

1. Giving thanks can make you happier https://www.health.harvard.edu/healthbeat/giving-thanks-can-make-you-happier. Accessed 2 Sent 2023
2. Lilian Jans-Beken , Nele Jacobs , Mayke Janssens , Sanne Peeters , Jennifer Reijnders , Lilian Lechner & Johan Lataster (2020) Gratitude and health: An updated review, The Journal of Positive Psychology, 15:6, 743-782, DOI: 10.1080/17439760.2019.1651888

8. LETTING GO OF EXPECTATIONS

1. E'lphistone, B, Whitehead, R. Bates, G. Letting go' and flourishing in study: An investigation of the indirect relationship between nonattachment and grades via psychological wellbeing, Learning and Individual Differences, Vol 78, Elsevier, https://doi.org/10.1016/j.lindif.2020.101847.
2. Sharon Martin, DSW, LCSW. Embrace your imperfections. https://www.psychologytoday.com/gb/blog/conquering-codependency/202102/embrace-your-imperfections.

ACKNOWLEDGEMENTS

Like so many things, a book is truly a project of collaboration in so many ways. While I may have put the words together, a multitude of others contributed feedback, thoughts and discussions that only added to the value of the book. To them, I am eternally grateful. All good things, I attribute to them, and any fault within these pages are all my own.

Many thanks to Sam, who designed the gorgeous, bright attractive cover. I love it!

Thank you also to the many early readers who spotted errors, helped perfect the prose and all in all, made the book better in so many ways

And to you, dear reader, thank you for joining me on this journey to finding all the joy we deserve in our lives.

ABOUT THE AUTHOR

Li-ling writes best, every morning at 4 am when the rest of her household is still asleep and the dog is too drowsy to keep begging for treats. This quiet time also helps her consolidate and solidify her never-ending thoughts and ideas for more books and such.

She writes non-fiction that borders self-development and new age beliefs. She writes of things that inspire, encourage and uplift her, in hopes of sharing that inspiration with the world at large. Her fiction books meanwhile, are an escape in which she daydreams that she too might be as brave, as out-going and as extroverted as many of her characters.

She enjoys beautiful walks, curling up with a good book, and time spent with family and friends. She lives with her family in Bath, UK and loves hearing from readers by email or social media. If you haven't already, sign up for her mailing list on her website lilingooi.com

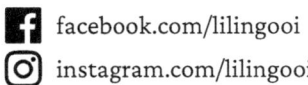

facebook.com/lilingooi
instagram.com/lilingooi

JOIN MY MAILING LIST

If you would like to stay up to date with my forth-coming books and projects, please sign up to my mailing list at lilingooi.com. I will only email when there is a new release or with exciting news.

Like you, I hate spam, so you can be assured that your email address is safe, will be kept private and will never be passed on to a third party. Also be assured that while I would be sad to see you go, you may unsubscribe from my mailing list at any time.

ALSO BY LI-LING OOI

Non-fiction

Joyful Living — Finding Joy in Little Things

A Year of Money and Abundance

Principles of X-ray Crystallography

Forth-coming titles

Non-fiction

Lighten the Load — Empowering Busy Moms to Let Go of the Mental Burden

Fiction

Secret Conversations — Lessons on Life and Living

PLEASE LEAVE A REVIEW

As an independently published book, every review (hopefully positive) helps this book get seen. I really hope you have enjoyed reading and learning from the knowledge and experiences shared in this book. If you liked it, I would be so very grateful if you could leave a review where you purchased the book so that it may encourage others to start on their journey to Joyful Living.

If you have thoughts or ideas on how anything could be better or improved upon, I would love to hear from you too. Please do leave me a message using the contact form on my website lilingooi.com/contact

COMING SOON
LIGHTEN THE LOAD: HELPING MOMS LET GO OF THE OVERWHELM

Motherhood is one of the most cherished roles in the history of all humanity. There is little that has not been attributed to the wondrous mother —from Mother Nature, keeper of this place we call home; to Mary, mother of God himself. Despite this reverence to the ultimate life-giving force, motherhood has undergone monumental changes over the course of time. From the role of the prehistoric mother who did all she could to shield her offspring from predators, to the modern mother constantly juggling between conference calls and parent-teacher meetings, the very essence of motherhood has always revolved around love, sacrifice, and a burning desire to provide the very best for one's children.

Today's mother, while free from the life-threatening challenges of her ancestors, faces pressures and burdens of an entirely different nature. In an era where the definition of success is ever-changing and often externally dictated, modern mothers find themselves straddling the ever blurry line between their individual desires and aspirations and a whole host of societal expectations. The developments of the modern world, while has made life significantly easier with it's many tools and gadgets, has also brought, mind-numbing, ceaseless digital chatter and visually curated slices of an idealised life, which adds layers of complexity to the maternal role.

Mothers are constantly bombarded with images of 'perfection' from social media, magazines, and television. There is an insidious undercurrent of messages implying that moms must not only be nurturing, but also career achievers, health gurus, master chefs, educators, and social coordinators. And while they chase these ideals, they must never appear overwhelmed, tired, or—God forbid—unhappy.

Sadly, the expectations don't just stop there. The modern mother is urged to provide her children with endless opportunities, from piano lessons and ballet classes to STEM programs and competitive sports. The fear of missing out on nurturing a potential prodigy is palpable. Yet, in the midst of all this, moms are also expected to maintain the perfect home environment where homemade meals abound, laughter rings, and where messes are merely aesthetic—a place where every corner of the home is Instagram-ready.

But here's the catch: while expectations soar, time doesn't expand and neither do emotional reservoirs. Burnout, anxiety, and a sense of inadequacy loom large for many, possibly every modern mom. There is a constant mental tallying of tasks, a silent clock ticking away, reminding mothers of all that they have yet to achieve, or worse, where they might be 'falling behind' even 'failing.'

In Lighten the Load, our purpose is to work together to unpack these burdens, dissect the sources of pressure, and offer practical solutions for empowerment. This book is a tribute to every mother who has felt the weight of modern expectations and seeks tools to lighten her load, find her joy, and forge a path that aligns with her own values, rather than those imposed upon her by society.

So, dear reader, as you dive into the chapters ahead, know that you are not alone in your feelings or experiences. This book aims to be your companion, your guide, and most importantly, a testament to the fact that being a 'perfect' mother is a myth. Being a present, loving, and authentic mother, on the other hand, is the ultimate truth.

Welcome to a journey of self-discovery, relief, and empowerment.

Onwards fellow mama,

Li-ling

www.ingramcontent.com/pod-product-compliance
Lightning Source LLC
Chambersburg PA
CBHW072057110526
44590CB00018B/3212